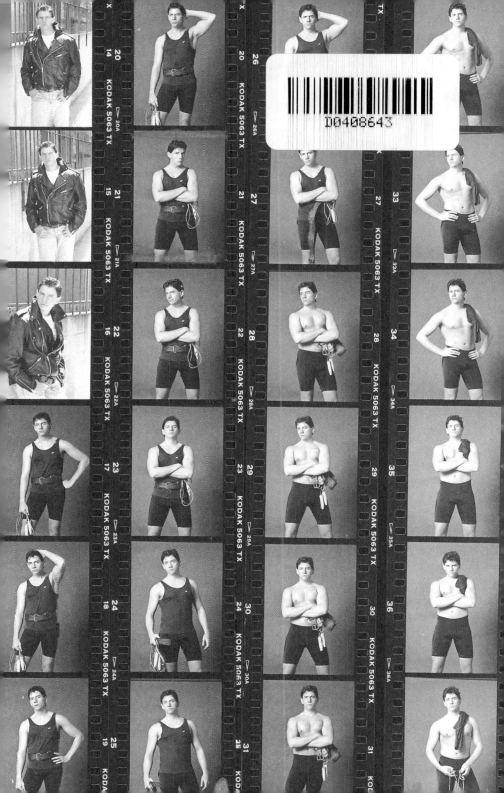

D0408643

WANNABE

WANNABE

A Hollywood Experiment

JAMIE KENNEDY

with

Ellen Rapoport

CITADEL PRESS
Kensington Publishing Corp.
www.kensingtonbooks.com

CITADEL PRESS BOOKS are published by

Kensington Publishing corp.
850 Third Avenue
New York, NY 10022

All Kensington titles, imprints, and distributed lines are available at special quantity discounts for bulk purchases for sales promotions, premiums, fund-raising, educational, or institutional use. Special book excerpts or customized printings can also be created to fit specific needs. For details, write or phone the office of the Kensington special sales manager: Kensington Publishing Corp., 850 Third Avenue, New York, NY 10022, attn: Special Sales Department; phone 1-800-221-2647.

CITADEL PRESS and the Citadel logo are Reg. U.S. Pat. & TM Off.

Figure on p. 18 courtesy of Robert Kennedy
Figure on p. 25 courtesy of E. Keyes
Figure on pp. 172–3 courtesy of Robbins Research International, Inc., San Diego, CA
Figure on p. 189 courtesy of Breakdown Services
Figure on p. 222 courtesy of Miramax
Figure on p. 227 courtesy of Pam Cole
Figure on p. 241 courtesy of WB Television Network
All other figures courtesy of the author's collection

First printing: August 2003

10 9 8 7 6 5 4 3 2 1

Printed in the United States of America

Library of Congress Control Number: 2003104614

ISBN 0-8065-2571-1

*To my parents, Bob and Josie, who gave me my
sense of humor and supported my journey
even when they didn't understand it*

Contents

WANNABE

Hating the Intro

I don't think anyone should write their autobiography until after they're dead.
—Samuel Goldwyn

I really hate writing this intro. Our editor said it had to be about a defining moment. My coauthor told me every one that I came up with was either too goofy or too depressing. It's an impossible question. I mean, I have a lot of defining moments in my life. Which one do you want? Was it when I was four, and I found my grandmother's dead body? Was it when I was seven, and my parents gave me a bag of coal for Christmas? Was it when I was ten, and I faked my first heart attack? Was it when I was eleven years old at Boy Scout camp, and my counselor told me he had a merit badge in tea-bagging? Was it when I was eighteen, and a girl I was fooling around with asked me if I wanted to know Satan? Was it during the LA Riots, when I watched a 7-11 get burned to the ground, then ran around the corner to warn a woman in Noah's Bagels that the looters were coming and she said, "They'll never come here. It's *Noah's*"? Was it during the second season of *JKX*, when I pulled a prank on a gangbanger and he threatened to kill me? Is that what you want to hear?

Our editor also said that the intro should let people know who I am. Who *am* I? Well, first and foremost, I'm a nice guy. Now, I could be all coy and self-deprecating, but this one thing I know is true. I really do care about you, my fellow human being. Why, you ask? Because I *am* you. I want *you* to be happy, because you are a reflection of *me*, and I want to be happy.

I'm also a massive liar. I will lie about anything, to anyone, at anytime, for any reason. Mainly because I don't want to hurt your feelings. And I don't want to be judged.

I'm intuitive, to the point where I can almost read your mind. It's not that I can, though. I just pay attention to you, whereas most people don't. You wear your thoughts on your sleeve. And you can't hide them very well.

I'm perverted. If you're attractive, I will probably climb on top of you and try to hump you.

I get scared a lot. Especially of being hurt physically.

I have issues with commitment.

I don't shower much. Showers take time and I don't want to waste it.

I am obsessive. I am manipulative. I am conniving. I like to laugh, sometimes at your expense. I am thoughtful. And I appreciate when you are too.

I am like a rubber band, physically. I am built like Big Bird. I am a dork. I always look like I'm stoned.

I am sensitive, and I get my feelings hurt often. I sometimes have a temper. I can cut you down verbally, to the point where you will cry, and I haven't even begun yet, YOU FUCKING COCKSUCKER.

To be honest, I don't know what I am. I am everything. And I am nothing. All I ever wanted was to matter.

1.

Growing Up a Kennedy

Happiness is having a large, loving, caring,
close-knit family in another city.
—George Burns

Kissing Cousins

People always want to know: what was it really like growing up a member of America's most potent political dynasty? The unprecedented power, the strain of ambition, the touch football games with Bobby and John John at Hyannisport? Unfortunately, I have no idea. I was raised by a different set of Kennedys—Bob and Josie of Upper Darby, Pennsylvania.

My mother, Josie, was born in Philadelphia. She grew up in an Irish Catholic family where money was tight but the Blessed Mother was always right. Grandma and Grandpa popped out kids like they were going out of style. They didn't stop until they got to seven. My mom's entire childhood was spent sleeping in a closet. Two other sisters had the room, but shared the bed. I guess my grandparents liked Josie the best.

According to my mother, her childhood was simple and happy. She says, "We never screamed at each other. We had sixty-four neighbors and knew every one of them, and we used to go to the playground to tap dance." And apparently Willy Wonka lived right around the corner in his magical house of chocolate.

My mother was a straight-A student, the valedictorian of her class of seven hundred. The family didn't have enough money to send her to college—my grandfather was supporting them on four thousand dollars a year. So when my mom graduated from high school, she had to get a job working as a junior stenographer for an ice cream company, making twenty-eight dollars a week. It was a rocky road.

My grandmother, Rose Maguire, was an Irish immigrant from Donegal, fresh off the boat from Ellis Island. She ruled her household with an iron fist. Her favorite dish to feed the brood was cabbage fried in bacon grease. They had it every Saturday for lunch. My mom absolutely hated it and told my grandma as much. Grandma told my mom that she had to eat it or starve. So my mom ate the cabbage and then threw up all over the table. The good part was that she never had to eat cabbage again. The bad part was that she lived in a house where the only way to avoid eating a food item was to vomit it up on everyone else.

My grandmother wanted all of her daughters to be nuns. My aunt Donna was the only one who went for it, though she quit after a few years. I think my mother actually wanted to be a nun as well, but then she found my father and gave up her dream of becoming the next Virgin Mary.

My father, Robert, had a very different upbringing. He was born in Knoxville, Tennessee, into a very wealthy, eccentric family, which might explain why he grew up to speak like a cross between Foghorn Leghorn and Colonel Sanders. The family owned a brewery, shoe stores, and a department store. My dad was surrounded with maids, butlers, chauffeurs, and a houseman named John Nelson. Unfortunately, that didn't last very long. My dad's father, an avid gambler, made some bad bets and lost most of the money. A mysterious flood at the brewery soaked up the rest of their savings. (I know—very Scooby Doo, but true.) My dad ended up supporting his parents at age seventeen.

My dad's brother was a prankster as a child. Once, when they were younger, he peed on a ham to make what he called "ham gravy." The family almost ate it, but John Nelson saved the day after he tasted the ham and realized it was baked in a little more than honey. Or, as he put it, "That's piss!"

———

Technically, my parents are cousins, which might explain a lot of things. That's right—our family tree has only one branch. Grandma Rose's brother married my dad's father's sister. My dad actually knew Grandma Rose from the time that he was four years old, because my grandmother visited my father's family in Tennessee once a year.

My dad hated school and dropped out to join the navy at seventeen. He asked my grandmother if she had a daughter for him to meet while he was on port in Philadelphia. The first daughter Grandma pimped out was my Aunt Donna, in her pre-nun stage. My father was pretty smooth. He wooed Donna with dinner, a movie, and a box of Jujubees. Then, he tried to hit it.

The next day, he left for the Mediterranean. Six months later, he got back to the Philadelphia naval port. He called up my grandmother.

"Where's Donna?" he asked. "Ah want another date."

"Sorry, Bob," Grandma said. "Donna joined the convent."

Apparently, my dad had quite a way with women.

"Huh," he said. "Well, who else you got?"

Grandma volunteered her middle daughter, Josie, my mother. Bob agreed, so Grandma told him to come around that night. They went out. After their date, they went back to Grandma Rose's house, where my mom invited my dad into her closet. Then he went to Europe for six months and wrote her letters on and off, coming back to see her when he was on leave. This went on for the next three years.

Finally, he got discharged from the navy. He went back to Philadelphia, to my grandmother's house. "Ah say, Josie," he said. "Ah say, I'm fixin' to make a move. You wanna do this?"

She said she had to ask her mother first. My grandmother told her that she liked Bobby and that was that. They got married when she was twenty-five. By the time my mom was thirty, she had four babies. She was a Fertile Myrtle. Now, I didn't come along until she was forty-one, and she only had one kid in her thirties. You do the math. That's right. I wasn't invited to the party. I was a big-ass mistake.

What's a Carpet Muncher?

My mother taught her kids to be polite at all costs, even if it meant sacrificing some honesty in the process. One time, our entire family went over to my aunt's house for Thanksgiving. She had cooked this enormous turkey. It was pink inside, still frozen, and had blood on it. I looked to my dad for guidance, but he just gave me a sour look and said, "Ah say, that turkey's still alive."

I complained, "Mom, it's frozen."

"Don't be rude," she said. "Just eat it."

"But it's bleeding!" I said.

"May I remind you that your aunt gave you a fifty dollar bond for your first birthday?"

My dad whispered, "Ah say, it's a goddamn ice cube."

My mom said, "Shhhh," and turned to my aunt. "It's delicious, Don. Very tasty."

I couldn't believe my mother was lying like this. "Mom," I said. "Everybody knows it's raw!"

She pulled my chair close to hers and glared at me. Through clenched teeth, she said, "Blood and ice will not kill you, but I might. Now eat the bird."

On the drive home, I whined to my mother, "How could you force me to eat a live turkey? I feel it crawling around in my stomach!"

"I don't know what turkey you ate, but mine was delicious," she said.

She has amazing powers of denial. Basically, if my mother believes something, it somehow becomes true. I remember being at a relative's house for dinner. The hostess had a woman with her who was clearly her girlfriend. On the drive home, my brother said, "Looks like we've got a carpet muncher in the family."

"What's a carpet muncher?" my mom asked. "I don't know anything about that."

"It means she's a lesbian," I piped in.

"Get out," she said. "She's a housemate. They're sharing a house. They're saving rent."

"Mom, they sleep in the same bed," I said.

"They're poor."

One year, my mom gave me a bottle of cologne for Christmas. It was called Exclamation! The bottle was shaped like an exclamation point. A few months later, I went on a date with a girl. She sniffed me, and then said, "You smell great. What is that?"

"It's Exclamation!" I said. "You like it? It comes in a cool bottle!"

"No way!" she said, looking at me oddly. "That's what *I'm* wearing!"

This was bad. Not only had I received women's perfume from my mother, but I had also *worn* it for the past two months. I told my mom what had happened.

"Get out," she said. "You're crazy."

"It's women's," I said.

"It's for men. Bruce Jenner wears it!"

She gave me two shirts the following Christmas. One of them was petite size.

———

My mother is big on appearances. Her worst fear is looking bad in front of our neighbors. Once, she got me a job driving her boss, a prominent lawyer, and his friend, the cardinal of Philadelphia, to the opera. When I dropped them off, I said, "Okay, I'll see you guys later." Then, I picked up a cheese steak and proceeded home.

The next day, when I saw my mother, she gave me a stern look and asked, huffily, "How did it go last night?

"Fine," I answered. "Why?"

"Is that right? Everything went well?"

"Yeah. . . . Why?"

"Uh huh . . ." She studied me.

"What?"

"My boss said you dropped him off and said, 'I'll see you guys later.'" She paused for dramatic effect, then shouted, "'YOU GUYS'?!"

"What's wrong with that?" I asked.

"You referred to them as YOU GUYS! They are *not* YOU GUYS! They are a *lawyer* and a *cardinal*. They are to be treated with utmost respect!"

"Well, how do I refer to them?"

"You refer to the cardinal as 'Your EXCELLENCY.'"

"Ah say, I don't see anything excellent about him," my dad piped in from the other room.

"YOU'RE NOT GETTING ANY ALLOWANCE!" my mom screamed back.

"AH DIDN'T DO NOTHIN'!" he pleaded.

Meanwhile, this is a woman who still, in 2003, refers to all Asian people as "The Chinese." It's not her fault, though—she's just fallen in with a bad crowd. Last year, I came home for Christmas and found my mom having a luncheon for some of her elderly friends. One of them asked, "Jamie, when you go on these auditions, do you have to go up against the blacks?" Clearly, she's a victim of peer pressure.

My mother's concern with our family's public image led her to monitor every avenue of potential embarrassment, including my personal life. When I was fourteen, I lost my virginity to a sixteen-year-old girl named Betty. That night, I came home with a ridiculous number of hickeys on my neck. I showed them to my father, thinking that because we were both men, he would appreciate my conquest. He took one look at my neck and immediately screamed for my mother. "Josie! Your son's been attacked by a vampire."

My mother looked at me and began to freak out. She

couldn't believe what I had done. "This is just awful," she said. "You look like you have scabies." All of a sudden, I didn't feel so sexy.

My parents had always said that I could talk to them about anything. Right then and there, I realized that "anything" did not include sex. After that, I definitely wasn't going to tell them that I spent the entire four-pump encounter trying to insert my penis into the top of this girl's pubic hairline while she kept laughing at me, saying, "Lower, dummy!"

The next day, my mother took me away to the beach for a week. She made me read a book called *Chastity is a Choice* and lay out in the sun until I got tan enough to cover up my hickeys.

Who Are You to Throw Out a Good Pencil?

When we were growing up, my mother got mugged a lot on the subway. One time she came home after having her purse snatched, wearing an expression of pride. She said, "I did it. I did it. I outsmarted these crooks."

"How?" I asked.

"Well," she said, "At the Thirty-eighth Street station, a kid asked me what time it was. Then, he tried to snatch my pocketbook, and the only reason he got it was because the strap broke—stupid, cheapie pocketbook. JC Penny is getting a call from me! Anyway, this tug of war ensued and I kicked the kid out the door of the train, but not before he got my purse."

"So, why are you so happy?" I asked.

"Because after I got mugged the last time, I started keeping my money in my sock. Haha! Little rat only got eleven cents! He tried to get me—I GOT HIM!"

Chalk one up for Josie! The only reason this happened was because she insisted on taking the subway to work. She never wanted to drive because parking was too expensive—and my mom was all about saving money. She was always on the lookout for a good deal. One time she came home with a huge bag of cat litter. I said, "Mom, we don't own a cat."

"I don't care," she said. "It was free."

We cut costs wherever we could. We never had real milk—just the powdered kind you mix with water. For years, I thought butter was called "company butter," because we only ate it when we had company. When it was just family, we used margarine, because it was cheaper.

We owned a moped instead of a second car, because insurance was too expensive. My mom was fifty-four years old, tooling around on this ridiculous little machine. One summer night, I was playing in the street with my friend Eric. All of a sudden, we heard this horrible ERRRRRRRRRRRRRRRRSCCCCCCC-CRRRRRRRRCHHHHHHH crashing sound. We looked over and saw the moped smashed into our trash cans, my mom facedown on the driveway. Eric said, "Dude, I think your mom just ate it." We ran over to help. She grumbled, "Damn clutch jammed. Rico the mechanic is getting a call from me!"

"Can we help you inside, Mrs. Kennedy?" my friend asked, reaching his hand out.

"You just worry about your own problems, Eric," she said. Then she stood up, wiped the garbage off of her, and went into the house.

She almost disowned me once for throwing out a pencil. I was cleaning up my room, and there was a half-used Ticonderoga 2 on my desk that I threw in the garbage can. I didn't think anything of it at the time. When I was done, my mom went through my trash and found the thing. She screamed at me, "WHO ARE YOU TO THROW OUT A GOOD PENCIL?"

Like I thought it was a *bad* pencil? And she was somehow taking the pencil's side?

Now I'm screwed because I do the same thing. If I go to a restaurant, I never valet the car. I just park on the street and end up walking ten blocks. I can never throw anything out. Recently, I took a shower with a girl. She looked over at my bath supplies and said, "What *are* those?" There were a bunch of soap-ends stacked in a neat pile. These little tiny slivers of soap. She started to throw them out. Before I could stop myself, I yelled at her, "WHO ARE YOU TO THROW OUT GOOD SOAP?"

A Cat With Wings

My father is a gentle giant—a simple, misunderstood man. When he was growing up, he was constantly harassed by everyone: his classmates, his siblings, the world. This might explain why he's devoted most of his adult life to outer space. From the time that he was twelve years old, my father had a vehement and steadfast belief in aliens. He remains confident that someday his own personal mother ship will come down to Earth and whisk him away.

His first alien encounter took place in the Smoky Mountains of Tennessee when he was twelve years old. He was climbing off his bike, next to a blackberry bush, when he heard a strange sound coming from the sky. According to his own description, he looked up and saw a huge, cigar-shaped figure, and said, "My God in heaven, that's a UFO." I asked him how he could be certain of what he saw. He said, "Because ever since that day . . . ah just loved blackberries."

My father believes that there are aliens living among us. They are reptilian, but disguised as human beings. Essentially, they have one layer of human flesh—peel that away and underneath you'll find a giant lizard. According to my father, there are good lizards and bad lizards. For example, the Queen of England is a good lizard. The Bush family is made up of bad lizards.

My father has many theories about how aliens have affected our everyday lives, and frankly, it's kind of hard to argue with some of them. For example, he gets very passionate when discussing the pyramids in Egypt. He asks, "How could a bunch of skinny Jews push huge bricks forty stories high in the sky? A UFO gotta do that." My father also believes that modern conveniences owe a huge debt of gratitude to extra-terrestrials. "How can you get pictures from your telephone? Man's not intelligent enough to create that. An alien had to design it. A Tic-Tac has only one calorie. Who can make something with so much flavor, so minty, but with only one calorie? Aliens."

―――――

My father's interest in other worlds isn't limited to outer space, but extends to the supernatural—he believes in spirits as well as aliens. One time I was sitting in our dining room, reading the newspaper. My father came down the stairs with a befuddled look on his face. I asked him what was wrong. He said, "Ah just saw a demon."

"Where?" I asked.

"On Momma's nightstand." ("Momma" is what my father calls my mother, despite the fact that she is not his mother. My mother calls my father "Daddy." So I guess in a sense they are not only cousins, but also each other's children.) I asked him how exactly this demon-sighting happened.

"Ah was on the phone and ah looked up and saw a cat on your mother's nightstand, but it was scaly and had wings, and ah thought, *Hey, ah've never seen a cat with wings,* so ah tried to catch it."

"And then what?" I asked.

"Ah chased it into the closet and then it went into another atmosphere."

Are you getting some sense of what my childhood was like? Try asking that man about the birds and the bees. Speaking of which, my dad has always seemed to think that he can communicate with the animal world as well. Maybe this is an offshoot of his whole alien/demon belief system. In any case, he had a very strange relationship with animals. Basically, he treated them like humans. He would talk to the cats that ran through our yard, saying, "Get outta here, cat. Go to your own home, goddamnit," as if they could understand him. A dog once peed on his flower bed, and my dad yelled at him, "You asshole! Why would you do that? Can't you see ah just got finished planting these azaleas? You stupid shit." He would argue with these animals as they were capable of rational thought—like the dog was going to go, "You know what, Bob? You're right. I was wrong. I should have used the toilet."

Because of his strong ties to the alien world, my dad has little hope for the human race. At one point he told me his best friend was a cigarette. This might be why he was always so protective of his smoking. One time, I took him to a huge supermarket called Ralph's. My dad felt compelled to light up a butt in the vegetable section. He was exhaling huge clouds of smoke while asking "Jay, is this organic broccoli?"

Some woman came up and said, "Sir, put that cigarette out right now or I will have you thrown out."

My dad said, "Excuse me lady, but do you own the supermarket? Is your name Ralph?" Then he just continued shopping, his best friend between his fingers.

My mother is tough as nails. Once, she tried to move my brother's motorcycle, kicked the kickstand up, and broke her foot. She walked on it for six weeks without even noticing it was broken. In contrast, my dad is kind of fragile. He used to drive from the suburbs deep into the heart of South Philadelphia on our moped, which didn't go more than thirty miles an hour. One time, when his wheel got caught on train tracks, he fell and bruised his arm. He immediately said, "Arm's gone," and filed for disability. He got a month off from work.

Maybe it wasn't that my dad was delicate, but that he hated his job. Once, he dropped forty pounds on his foot so he could take the summer off. The idea struck him while he was moving a lead brick. He looked around, made sure the supervisor couldn't see anything, then let it fly. He came home, so happy, and said, "Jay, looks like you're not the only guy with a summer vacation. Ah broke my foot . . . in two places! Ah'm out for twelve weeks!"

My dad's favorite thing to do instead of working was to sit in the living room for hours on end and stare into space, with a nice peaceful countenance about him. He'd put away probably a pack and a half of cigarettes during this time—and then random thoughts would start to come into his head. He'd need my input for all of them. "All right, Jay," he'd say. "Ah say, today is Monday. All right, so now, yesterday was a Sunday. And on Friday, we went to McDonald's, right? Now did ah have a hamburger or a cheeseburger that day? Your momma's a Klingon. No, ah think ah had Chicken McNuggets. Ah can't remember. Maybe it was Filet-O-Fish. Jesus was an alien."

Born Into a Prank

In retrospect, it's no surprise that I ended up doing what I do— hiding in closets and pulling pranks on poor, unsuspecting people. I was born into a joke, people. My entire life is a prank.

Try this one on for size: December 1977. I was seven years old. My mother and father kept telling me how naughty I'd been all year. Every time I would act up, they'd say, "Just be careful, or you might get coal in your stocking." As the weeks drew closer, it turned into, "You know, Santa's not coming for you this year. He's gonna fly right over our house."

I didn't take them seriously. In fact, I didn't even know what that meant. The week before Christmas, I was so excited that I got up every day at six in the morning to look under the tree. Like clockwork, my mom would say, "Whatcha doing? It's not Christmas yet. It's Tuesday, ya brat."

Finally, the big day arrived.

I woke up, ran downstairs, and looked under the tree. Everyone had presents waiting for them—everyone except me. I searched the entire room, finding nothing, and then went over to where my stocking hung. Inside the stocking was a little bucket of coals. I reached in and tried to see if the real present was hidden under the coal, but there was nothing there. I rummaged around under the tree again. Zilch.

I ran around like a headless chicken, sobbing, then sped upstairs to wake my parents. I asked them, how they could do this to me? How could they be so mean? They just acted like they were asleep. I got mad and screamed, "I demand to speak to Santa!" Then they started to laugh. Finally, my mother sat up, rolled her eyes, and said, "Can't you take a joke? Your presents are on the porch. Geez."

I ran outside and found a huge bag of toys. It was more than I had ever gotten before, but I was still too shaken to appreciate it. I suppose they gave me coal because they really wanted me to take a moment and think, *Gee, I guess I have been bad.* But all I could think was, *How could anyone give another person coal? It's awful!* The worst part was that my parents didn't even seem that sorry—they were just disappointed that I had ruined their joke by being such a crybaby.

Hey, Is That Jamie Kennedy with a Gorilla?

I have a pretty large family—four sisters and a brother. They all have their own eccentricities.

One sister thought that Americans were programmed to believe in strict gender roles—that our criteria for considering a trait feminine or masculine was just a response to cultural conditioning. To counteract this, she grew out her armpit hair. I'm not talking about a little hair. This was straight, jet black, Italian goomba hair. She recently took me out for my birthday in Malibu and kept raising her arm to get the waitress's attention. Every time she moved, a huge animal would emerge from her armpit. People were staring at us, probably wondering, *Hey, why is Jamie Kennedy with a gorilla?*

Another sister was a little tight with a buck. One Christmas, she was going out with a watch dealer, so she gave everyone Swatch watches. I looked in my stocking and noticed that it was empty. I asked her, "Why did everyone get a watch but me?"

"Because you owe me a hundred and fifty dollars," she said.

"So?"

"So instead of getting you a present, I took the seventeen-dollar watch price off your tab."

"But those watches are like forty-five bucks," I said.

"I know, but I got them wholesale. Merry Christmas!"

My brother was a tad socially awkward. He didn't really know how to shake hands, so when he met someone, there was always drama. He jiggled their hand really quickly and then looked at the ground. Then he would proceed to hock up a loogie and swallow it. If a beautiful girl walked by, he'd randomly blurt out things like, "Look at her tits," as if he were a Tourette's patient. Recently, he crashed my car because he felt that I was ignoring him. It would have been so much easier if he'd just asked for a hug.

From: Robert kennedy robertfkennedy@earthlink.net
Date: Tue, 05 Mar 2002 00:37:14 - 0500 (pst)
To: JamieK@aol.com
Subject: Dad is spooked!

Mom said dad is getting paranoid about all sorts of things. He said he found $13 in his pocket that came from outer space. Are you still pissed about the car?

I'm in the Soup

My neighborhood was home to a lot of oddballs. The man who lived three doors down hadn't cut his grass in over twenty years. The woman across the street was a devout Catholic who claimed to have seen the Virgin Mary in a piece of Swiss cheese. By far, the oddest was our next-door neighbor, an elderly lady who took enormous pride in her lemon tree. One year, the tree suddenly stopped sprouting lemons. This woman bought plastic lemons and tied them to the tree. I remember looking out at her yard in the dead of winter, a foot of snow on the ground, thinking, *That tree is amazing. Nothing can stop those lemons.*

This kind of stuff provided the backdrop to my childhood, which was bizarre and ordinary all at once. I don't really remember too much about being really young. I remember taking a shit in my crib and throwing it against the wall. I remember playing in the yard, getting scared and taking a shit in my pants. I remember going to the circus and being fascinated by an elephant taking a huge shit. Why do I just remember the shitty times?

My first conscious thought was at age two. I was walking on these bricks outside our house with my best friend. We were playing a game called turtle soup. The object was to stay on the bricks because if you fell, you'd go into the soup, which was supposed to be all hot and bubbly. Then I fell and I thought, *Whoa, I'm in the soup. The turtles are gonna eat me.* As I was standing there, I started thinking, *Wait a minute. I'm not in the soup. I'm standing on the sidewalk. How did I get here? Who am I? What am I doing with my life?* It was like feeling my brain turn on. I ran into the house, totally disoriented.

I heard my sister call our grandmother "Grandma," so I called her "Grandma" too. For the longest time, I didn't even know what Grandma meant. I just copied everybody. I used to lick our cat, because I saw it lick itself. One day my sister saw me licking it, and said, "No, Jamie. You pet it." That's kind of how my life has been since then—like running with the bulls in Pamplona. I just go where the current directs me.

As I grew older, I became scared of everything. I was scared of the ocean, scared of other kids, scared of cars. I definitely wasn't equipped to be macho. I was a constant crier. I remember bawling my eyes out on the first day of school. I was so upset, because it was raining. And because the school was made out of this old wood, which was dark brown and cold. And because the only snack available was a pretzel. Sounded scary. More crying. In fact, I cried every day for, like, the first two weeks. I was such a momma's boy—I needed someone to hold my hand. I'm still sort of like that. (And to this day I have a weird aversion to wood—it depresses me.)

From age six on, this was basically my life: I would go to school, get scared, cry, daydream, come home, and from four to eleven P.M., sit in the basement and watch TV. I had milk and Chips Ahoy cookies and then dinner, all in front of the television. My mother kept her office in the basement, so from the time I was six until I was about seventeen, I spent every afternoon watching my family parade into my mother's office and request one thing or another. My brother would go in, hock up a loogie, swallow it, and leave. My dad would shuffle in and try to convince my mom to raise his allowance, then shuffle out, defeated. My oldest sister would storm in, holler at my mother for taking her out of art class when she was five, and then stomp out of the room. My other sister, who changed her lifestyle every week, would amble by, and announce that she was no longer a born-again Christian but a vegan—and did anyone want to try some fresh-baked twelve-grain banana-nut-seaweed bread?

All my brothers and sisters were very smart and well edu-cated; every single one of them ended up with a masters degree or a Ph.D. The thing is, they were completely removed from popular culture. So as they would leave my mom's office, they'd look at me on my couch, watching television, and shake their heads, saying, "Jamie, why don't you read a book?"

"No thanks," I'd say. "I'd rather watch Jack Tripper fool Mr. Furley into thinking he's gay one more time."

"Who's Mr. Furley?" they'd ask. "That guy from up the street?"

"Never mind."

Looking back, I can't believe my mother and father let me get away with watching seven hours of TV a day. That's the great thing about being the youngest. By the time your parents get to you, they don't have any energy left for child-rearing.

Television really shaped my personality and my outlook on the world. I spent my formative years in front of that box. I knew all the jingles: "You're not fully clean unless you're Zestfully clean!" "Time to make the donuts, the donuts." "Where's the Palmolive, Madge? You're soaking in it!" I knew them all! John Ritter was my first role model. I used to watch *Three's Company* constantly and think that was the way life should be—you live with two hot girls, have a wacky best

friend named Larry, and hang out at the Regal Begal at night.
I was so stupid that I thought it was like a documentary about
someone's life—I didn't know that it was a TV show or what a
TV show even was. All I knew was that the TV was something
you turned on and stuff came out at you. I wasn't so naïve as to
think that John Ritter actually lived inside my TV, but I did
think that television people existed in an alternate universe
where everyone was tan and good-looking and fun.

TV let me see the world as this beautiful place. Then, the
world let me down. I didn't learn valuable life lessons in thirty
minutes and things never wrapped up in the end. I hated that.
I wanted to live in a sitcom. In fact, I still do. Nothing makes
me happier than lying in bed, eating pizza, and watching TV.
My dream is to be so rich that I can live out the rest of my life
in front of a television, watching reruns.

Like an Episode of Little House on the Prairie

When I was growing up, I was the only emotional kid in my
family, and everyone looked at me like I was a lunatic. I always
felt like James Dean in that scene from *Rebel Without a Cause*,
where he screams, "You're tearing me apart!" Like I was doing
takes for a camera that wasn't there.

I used to get very upset at our dinner table, because no
one ever took my problems seriously. In an effort to get attention, I would often throw green beans against the wall and
shout, "You're not listening to me!" My mom would just say,
"Oooh, Jamie threw his beans" in a sarcastic tone. This would
make me even more upset. She'd shake her head and say, "Get
ahold of yourself." Then I'd have a crying fit.

When these fits would happen I would run to my room,
work myself into a genuine frenzy, and cry uncontrollably. My
sister would follow me upstairs, see me upset, and then start to

cry. Then, my father would come in, say, "Jay, ah hate to see you like this, boy," and proceed to lose it. Finally, my mother would enter the room and stare at all of us. She'd stand there, her exterior very tough. Slowly, she would start to crack, but she wouldn't go all the way. She was going to keep it together. Finally, my dad would grab her and say, "LET GO, WOMAN! BREAK! CAN'T YOU SEE YOUR SON'S IN PAIN?" The scene would end with the four of us, standing in a huddle, crying together.

It was so melodramatic. Like an episode of *Little House on the Prairie*. But in those few moments, I felt great. Like everyone finally understood me. That's why, to this day, the only way I feel I can get attention is by crying. Because when people see guys cry, it wigs them out.

My parents were baffled by this behavior—I was the last kid and no one had shown as much emotion before. One day, my father decided to have a talk with me.

He said, "Jay, ah never realized how sensitive you were."

I said, "Dad, don't your feelings ever get hurt?"

"Sure," he said. "But you gotta keep 'em in check. It's like when ah'm out there in the garden, and ah've done all my trimming and pruning and dug all the weeds up and ah got the rhododendron bush looking real pretty and nice. And then . . ."

"Yeah?"

His voice got hushed, "Keith, that goddamn five-year-old kid from next door, comes trudging through the flowerbed and tramples on my hours of hard work, looking for his goddamn ball. Sure, ah get my feelings hurt. Ah want to take a hatchet and put it in his head. And maybe take it out and do it again. But ah can't. Ah'd go to jail. And then, where would Momma be? Married to a jailbird!"

"Dad, I just cry," I said.

"Right," he said. "Same thing."

Making Friends with Your Battery

Starting from the time that I was seven or eight, I had semi-constant, sharp chest pain. It felt like I was being stabbed by a needle. I'd complain to my mom, but she wouldn't believe me. "It's gas," she'd say. "Stop crying wolf." Eventually, I just stopped noticing it.

One day in fifth grade, I was really bored in math class. I decided to make myself hyperventilate so I could get out of there. I started wheezing and breathing rapidly. The teacher panicked and took me to the nurse. The nurse checked me out and said that something was wrong, but she didn't know what. She sent me to a doctor. The doctor said the same thing and sent me to the emergency room. I thought, *Man, my acting is really good.* The emergency room doctors referred me to a specialist at Children's Hospital of Philadelphia. There, the specialist found something.

"What???" I screeched. "No! I was acting! There can't be something there!"

"You were?" my mom asked.

"I just didn't want to do math," I said.

"No," the specialist said. "You have a congenital heart block."

"Oh God! It's real?"

"Very. We have to start running tests."

They did. And I started failing them, miserably.

In these exercise stress exams, I would walk on a treadmill and do pushups while doctors monitored my electrocardiogram, heart rate, and blood pressure. No matter what I did, I couldn't get my heart rate up to normal, which was about one hundred seventy-five beats per minute. Once it went all the way up to one hundred twenty, then suddenly dropped to thirty-eight. I felt weak, like I was going to pass out.

They told me that I might have to have a pacemaker put in my chest. I didn't know what a pacemaker was, but I knew it wasn't normal. I hated the thought of having some foreign object in my body or a machine responsible for my life. I started trying to beat the tests. But each time, the results got worse and worse.

I knew the day of reckoning was approaching, because my mother started surreptitiously leaving all these pamphlets from the doctor's office around the house. One was called "Jeffrey's Little Pacemaker." Another was "Making Friends with Your Battery." These pamphlets were designed to make people feel better, but instead they just depressed me. They featured these happy little pictures of people doing the most mundane things, with a drawing of a pacemaker in their chest. The caption read: "Things you can do with your pacemaker: Make toast! Mow the lawn! Feed your domesticated animal!" I didn't even want to do those things *without* a pacemaker.

Then, I read one that mentioned sex, maintaining that after the operation, one could enjoy a healthy, happy sex life, with plenty of erections. I was so relieved. I didn't even know what sex was, but I was already looking out for my future.

Finally, when I was fourteen years old, the doctor said that it was time. When I went into the hospital, I realized how miniscule my problems were, compared to everyone else's. The other kids were in really bad shape. Half of the kids in my ward had cancer. One boy had excess fluid in his brain. His head was three times the size of mine. The eight-year-old in the room across from me was having his third open heart surgery. This kid's chest had more staples in it than a telephone pole.

After I came back from the operation, my roommate, this really nice young kid, was gone. "Where's Brian?" I asked the nurse.

"He passed this morning."

It was a total reality check.

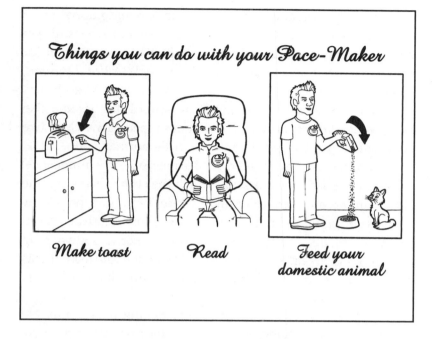

Things you can do with your Pace-Maker

Make toast *Read* *Feed your domestic animal*

There were three other pacemaker recipients on my floor: a four-week-old baby, a girl so freaked out by the surgery that she tried to cut the pacemaker out of her chest, and a twenty-year-old guy named Elvis. Elvis had two pacemakers in his chest, one on each side. And he wouldn't quit smoking.

I asked him, "Why don't you stop?"

He said, "You can't stop the King."

I was supposed to be in the hospital for only three days, but for some reason my heart was beating irregularly, so I had to stay for over three weeks. I remember sitting in my hospital bed and watching *Friday Night Videos*. Madonna's "Material Girl" video played all the time, and I kept thinking that I wanted to be the material girl. She had everything, and I had metal in my chest.

After the operation, I was really upbeat and happy. Then, the denial passed and I became depressed and resentful. Up until that point I had been just like everybody else (except for my left nipple, which wasn't fully developed). All of a sudden, I had a label. I was the "Don't tackle him, he's got a bad heart" kid. I had to wear heart monitors to school that looked like giant walkie talkies, and have electrodes taped to my chest like the Bionic Boy. I thought I could never be normal again.

Getting the pacemaker made me lose my innocence. Before that, I used to constantly watch the show *CHiPs*. All the kids on it were tan and buff and blonde. I thought that's how life was supposed to be. You surf, you get tan, you drink Pepsi. Health problems? What's that? The pacemaker was a wake-up call—it made me face my own mortality at age fourteen. It was like I finally discovered that I was a living, breathing organism. I was vulnerable.

This was when the clock started ticking on my life. No matter what I was doing or how much fun I was having, in the back of my mind I was always thinking, *I could die tomorrow.*

Eventually, I learned how to make the pacemaker work for me. I found I could get what I wanted through sympathy. For example, I loved fast food, but my mother always refused to buy it for me. We'd be driving on our moped, making conversation, when we'd pass a McDonald's. "Oooh, Mom! Can I have two all beef patties, special sauce, lettuce, cheese, pickles, onions on a sesame seed bun?" I'd ask. "Please?"

"Forget it. That place is a rip off," she'd say.

"A Quarter Pounder?"

"No! Absolutely not."

And that was the end of that. But after the surgery, I realized that I could take a new persuasive tack. We were driving on the moped again, and passed the same McDonald's. "Oooh, Mom! Can I have—"

"*No!*" she said. "You're going to have your dinner soon."

"Okay, fine," I said.

Then I waited thirty seconds. Out of nowhere, I screamed, "OWWWWWWWWW!!!!!! MY CHEST HURTS!!!!" I clutched my heart and moaned in pain, almost falling off the moped.

My mother immediately let the clutch out and stopped. She asked, frantically, "What's wrong?"

"Can't . . . breathe," I croaked.

"What can I do to help?" she asked.

I coughed and tried to whisper. "McNuggets? And maybe a milkshake?" She turned the moped around.

It got to the point where we'd pass by a McDonalds, I'd touch my chest, and she'd immediately pull over and order me whatever I wanted. I was always a little ashamed of myself, but also proud of my acting skills.

Jamie Kennedy: Horse Cobbler

I never gave much thought to the future until my junior year of high school, when our school hosted a "Career Day." Our guidance counselor sat us down for a one-on-one consultation, after which we were supposed to pick a career. We each got about ten minutes with the guy. It doesn't seem like much, but it was long enough to scare the crap out of me.

"Make sure you pick something you really like," he told me. "Because you'll be doing it for the next forty or fifty years."

WHAT?! That was an eternity. I asked him if there was any way to change your career after you'd gotten started.

"Not likely," he said. "Because then you have to go back to school and it's a big hassle. For example, let's say you want to be a horse cobbler. There are only two horse cobbling schools in the United States, and both of them don't accept students who are over thirty."

"Well, I don't think I'm going to be shoeing horses for a living," I replied.

He considered me grimly. "You never know."

That freaked me out. I knew then and there that I had to get my life together, or else I'd wake up twenty years from now to find myself trimming some Clydesdale's toenails.

Acting had always been an idea in the back of my mind, but I had never seriously considered it. In my town, acting in school plays was for the theatre geeks. My friends were way too cool for that, and I was scared that they'd make fun of me if I pursued the performing arts. I had no acting mentors. I did have a great uncle who used to dance on street corners with a hat. But he was also convinced that the eyes of potatoes were watching him, so he wasn't exactly the best role model.

I started studying books about actors. When I read Bill Cosby's autobiography, a few things struck me. He wrote, "Don't do this unless it's the only thing you can do, and if you don't do it you will be rejecting every bone, every muscle, every nerve in your body." This was *exactly* how I felt. It was such a relief to know that I wasn't the only one who had this mass of frenzied, undirected ambition. Suddenly, it seemed possible.

I started thinking. Bill Cosby was twenty-five when he began his comedy career. He was from Philly and dead broke. And so I reasoned to myself: I'm from Philly and I'm dead broke. But I'm only seventeen. When Bill Cosby started, he was paying one dollar a day for a shower, squatting in a rat-infested apartment building, and making five dollars a week as an emcee. I thought, *I have a seven-year window to get to that level. I can definitely be making five dollars a week by that time.*

I realized that acting could bring me all that I wanted out of life. For example, I wanted to see the world. If I got a cool acting job in, say, Tunisia, I'd get to travel, plus I'd get paid for it. Also, I'd be better able to take in my surroundings because my work probably wouldn't be too strenuous. Then, I considered the women. It's not like I was meeting too many girls in my all-boys Catholic school. But if I were an actor, I could meet actresses, who were some of the most desirable women in the world. I'd be an actor, and therefore also highly desirable. In fact, I could actually travel the world and *simultaneously* have affairs. While getting paid! My mind was made up.

As high school drew to an end, my mom started to get on my case about college, but that was the last thing I wanted to do. To me, college is such a waste of time—unless you're looking to get date raped. I was only interested in acting. My mother was disappointed, but reluctantly agreed, hoping that I would get it out of my system.

I started taking classes at Delaware County Community College a few months after graduation. I chose two classes I was interested in—acting and cooking—plus math and English, which were required. Within weeks, I had dropped out of everything but acting and cooking. Then, I got into a fight with my cooking teacher. He was pontificating about what it takes to make brilliant omelettes.

I raised my hand and asked, "What's the big deal? I mean, eggs are eggs."

"Whoa!" he said. "I don't know about you, son, but when I leave this world, I want to be remembered for something."

Yeah, join the club. But . . . eggs?! Right, that's certainly making a mark on the world. My headstone could read, "Here lies Jamie Kennedy. His flan was off the hook."

I dropped that class the next day. All that remained was acting, which I loved. I had a great teacher, Theresa Donohue. She was my first true mentor in acting; she believed in me and pushed me to get better. After I performed my final scene for the class, Theresa asked to speak with me privately. She told me, "You can do this. You have talent." I got an A in her class, which made my average for the semester a 4.0, because all my other credits were invalid. I'd had my first taste of success— and it was better than I could have imagined.

2.

Extra Crazy

Insane people are always sure that they are fine.
It is only the sane people who are willing to
admit that they are crazy.

—Nora Ephron

Mr. Williams Is a Very Shy Man

My interest in professional extra-dom began at seventeen, thanks to my friend's mother, June, a local actress/ semi-celebrity. June had once done a Jiffy Lube television commercial with Bill Bergey, a former star Philadelphia Eagles player. I was very intimidated by her. In my mind, she was as big as Loretta Lynn. I told her once that I wanted to be an actor. "Don't do it," she said. "You're in for a lifetime of disappointment."

June was an extra in Robin Williams's movie *Dead Poets Society*, which was filming in Delaware. She knew I wanted to be an actor, so she called me up and asked if I wanted to be an extra.

"What's that?" I asked.

"Extras are the people who walk around the stars while they're doing their scenes. They create the atmosphere. You'll be in the movie."

"Definitely!" I said. I was so excited.

I met her at her house at four A.M. the next day, and we all went to Delaware: me, June, and her son. When we got there, June got jobs for both of us right away, in a scene where Robert Sean Leonard performs in a play. We were going to play audience members. Then a production assistant took me to get a short crew cut—the movie was set in the fifties. When the hairdresser finished, I asked her how much I owed. She just laughed and said, "Nothing, sweetie." I couldn't believe it. The night before, I was working at Domino's. Now I was on a set with Robin Williams, getting my hair cut for free.

You have to understand that, for me, the experience of being on a movie set for the first time was the equivalent of going to Mars. It was just something that I never knew existed. I mean, when I watched movies, I just knew whether I liked them or not. I didn't know how they were made. I didn't know that they shot the same scene twenty times from five different angles. I didn't know that stars used huge trailers to sleep in while they were waiting for their next shot. I didn't even know that there was food on the set. There was a guy walking around with a tray, offering everybody fruit and sushi, whatever the hell that was. I was used to working jobs where, if you wanted to eat, you had to steal the food. And you had somebody constantly looking over your shoulder, barking orders at you. Here, you were your own boss.

I thought I had found paradise on earth. A job that provided easy money (fifty dollars a day!), all the food I could eat, and professional hair maintenance. And on top of all that, all I had to do was stand around. I was doing nothing and getting paid for it. THIS was show business. What more could a person possibly want out of life?

All of a sudden, I spotted Robin Williams. He was just there, walking around, like any other ordinary person. It was *so bizarre.* I think it's always weird seeing someone famous for the first time. It's like seeing an extra-terrestrial. You never quite believe they're real, but then there they are, standing right in front of you. You just don't comprehend that they spend their days doing what you do, like walking around or eating a bagel.

Anyway, I developed this really strong need to speak to Robin Williams. But every time I got close, he would just walk by me super-fast. My friend and I came up with a plot. We decided that when Robin walked by us the next time, we would shout, "Hey Mork! Nanoo Nanoo!" Clearly he had never heard that one before. It would stop him dead in his tracks. Unfortunately, after a few very loud "HEY MORK"s the producers made an announcement warning the extras, "Please *do not* approach Mr. Williams. He is a *very* shy man."

My fellow extras were fascinating to me, primarily because I never had deep or even particularly long conversations with people of other ages or other cultures before. My friends were other pimply-faced, sixteen-year-old, Irish-Catholic white kids, just like me. Here, I was hanging out with old Chinese men, young black girls, middle aged women, gay guys, and Indians (sounds like a porno). And here, we had something in common—we all loved the free fruit.

This was the first time that I truly felt like I belonged somewhere. Every emotion I had been taught to suppress was welcomed and celebrated in this new environment. It was as though my whole life had been leading up to this experience.

This was IT. This was the dream. This was Hollywood. I mean, it was Delaware, but it was close enough.

An Extra What?

I had now done as much as I could with my acting career from Pennsylvania. I needed to go forward. I went in my mom's room and told her my news. I was moving to Los Angeles . . . to become a professional extra.

She shook her head and asked, "An extra what?" I explained that I was going to make a living walking behind people on movie sets, weaving in and out of crowd scenes. "Well, where's the career in that?" she asked, "What about benefits?"

I told her I had it all planned out. "I'll start as an extra, but then maybe the director will notice me and like my face and tell the star to shout at me in a scene. And if he does that, then my pay will be bumped up to, like, two hundred fifty dollars, and then I'll be a *featured* extra. Then, if the director likes the way I react to the star's shout, he could give me a line to shout back. Then I could make six hundred for the day. From there, it's only a matter of time until I work my way up to a recurring role as a wacky neighbor on a sitcom. Then I'll get paid, like, a thousand bucks a day. After that, what do you need?"

Although I didn't mention it at the time, I was secretly modeling myself after Joe Isuzu. I heard that he'd segued from extra work to those Isuzu commercials to *Empty Nest*. If I could just get my face in the background of *one* commercial, the world would be my oyster.

My mom just stared at me, like I was one of the aliens my dad talked about. Things were getting shaky. I tried to appeal to my mom's love of higher education, saying, "After I get out there, maybe I can go to an acting school."

"How much is that?" she asked.

"I don't know. I think about five thousand dollars a year," I said.

"Hmrph," she grumbled, "Well, do they have job placement?"

That's how out of touch my mom was. I mean, it was acting school. It's not like they had a human resources department who would say, "So you want to be an actor? What do you like, movies, television, or theater?"

"Movies, I guess."

"Great. How would you feel about a three-picture deal at Disney?"

"I don't know, man. *Goofy*?"

"Maybe you'd prefer to have NBC develop a sitcom for you? The most important thing is for you to be happy. 'Cause you know what? Hollywood needs *you*."

She went on, asking me what I was going to do for money in the meantime. I said, "I'll get a job."

"Oh!" she said, as a burst of inspiration hit her. "Why don't you work at Wienerschnitzel in Orange County and live with your sister?"

I said, "Do you know what's in Orange County, Ma? Oranges! You can't go out after nine P.M."

"Jamie," she sighed. "You just don't understand this world. There's a process. You work forty hours a week. You pay your phone bill, your electricity, your car, and your food. You go to church and you buy your clothes and you pay your taxes. Then, after all that, if you still have enough energy, you try to become an actor."

I knew that she loved me very much and only wanted the best for me. She just didn't understand what I was trying to do. Her plan might have worked really well in the forties. But it was not the way to become an extra!

———

A week before I left for California, I saw June at Pathmark.

"So, you're really doin' it, huh?" she said to me. "You're moving out to LA?"

"I am," I said.

She nodded. As I turned to walk away, she yelled out after me, "Jamie! Don't you know that you've got to be Ricky Schroeder to make it out there?"

I just smiled and nodded. But in my mind, I was picking up green beans and throwing them at her head.

If You Look Closely You Can See My Earlobe

My sister, the stingy stocking stuffer, had been living in Huntington Beach for a few years, working at McDonnell Douglas. When I came out to LA, she picked me up from the airport and took me back to her apartment in Orange County. I remember driving down the freeway, just looking around in a daze, taking it all in. It was all so open and sprawling: the eight lanes of cars, the huge expanse of sky, the ocean just to my right. I had grown up feeling claustrophobic, boxed-in. This was like being on a giant race track.

Even the most banal places were exotic to me. The supermarket was insane, as big as a football field, with seventy-foot ceilings and the brightest lights I'd ever seen. The vegetables were so fresh and so green—they went on for miles. They had carrot juice. I'd never even known you could get juice from a carrot before. The place was open all night. I could get

Lucky Charms at two in the morning if I wanted to. And there were blondes in heels everywhere. The whole thing was mind-blowing.

I wanted to break into Hollywood, but I didn't know how. So I decided to let my fingers do the walking. I picked up the yellow pages and went to work. I looked under "Stars"—nothing. "Celebrities"—nothing. "Actors"—boom. A listing for an extras' agency in Hollywood. I called for information. The receptionist said, "It costs thirty-six dollars to sign up. Once you join, we'll call you every day with potential jobs."

"Really? It's that easy?" I asked.

"Yeah," she muttered and hung up on me. I got my sister to drive me out to Hollywood. By the time we got to the agency, I was so excited that I was almost bouncing off the walls. The woman behind the desk just stared at me, bored. "Membership costs forty-dollars," she said.

"But I thought it was thirty-six!"

"There's a four-dollar processing fee."

All I had on me was my thirty-six dollars. My sister didn't have any money on her either.

"Can't you spot me four bucks?" I asked the woman.

"Nope."

I pleaded with her, "C'mon lady, this is my dream. I just moved to LA. Can't you let it slide?"

She scowled at me. "Come back Monday when you have four more dollars."

"Lady," I said. "I could be dead by then." She didn't seem to have a problem with that.

After we left, my sister said, "You should stay up here. It's time for you to get into the biz."

"But why?" I asked.

"It would be good for you. Plus my place is too small."

"But I only have thirty-six dollars."

She pulled up next to the Hollywood YMCA and said, "That'll buy you five nights here, easy."

"What about my stuff?" I asked.

"I'll bring it up this weekend," she said, unlocking my door. "Have fun!" Then she drove off.

I was really upset about the extras' agency situation, but I resolved to make it work, somehow. But before I got back to the agency, I learned something about the kinds of people who become professional extras—they're extra crazy.

The next night, I had my epiphany. I was sitting in a diner near the YMCA, reading Joan Rivers's autobiography. After the waiter took my order, he noticed the book in my hand. "Are you trying to be an actor?" he asked.

"Yeah," I said.

"That's what I do," he said.

"Really?" I asked. *One day in LA and I was already making contacts!* I was so excited.

"I have four movies coming out," he said.

"Wow! What are you waiting tables for?" I asked him.

"Well, I still have to keep my day job," he replied.

"But you're doing four movies?"

"Yeah," he said proudly. "I've already done a ton of stuff. In *Mannequin*, I'm the guy that Kim Cattrall waves to. When she's on the back of Andrew McCarthy's motorcycle, she waves at me. I was *featured*."

"So you're an extra."

"No," he said, "I'm in atmosphere. I'm a background artist."

"Okay . . ." I said. This guy sounded like me when I was talking to my mom, just one level crazier.

"You may have also seen me in *Ghost Busters*," he continued. "The library scene. I was the guy that Dan Akroyd walked by. I was in study carrel number three."

"Oh yeah. Yeah, yeah," I said, not wanting to offend him.

"I was in *Crocodile Dundee*. Remember the part where he pulled out the knife? Well, if you look real close, that's my earlobe."

This guy was like the Ghost of Christmas Future. Was I going to struggle to become an extra, and end up working in some diner ten years from now, bragging about how my knees had once done a scene with Mel Gibson? There had to be another way in.

I picked up my Joan Rivers book and searched for guidance.

3.

Working It

All paid jobs absorb and degrade the mind.
—Aristotle

Seating the Stars

At the YMCA, I slept on foam egg crates in a room with twenty other guys, mostly stinky Swedes with huge backpacks and *Let's Go Hollywood* guides. I picked the egg crates because they were the cheapest—eight dollars a night. The beds were twenty.

The first day, I walked for miles down Hollywood Boulevard. This was right at the beginning of summer, so the street was completely packed with people. It was total sensory overload. The first surprise was how rundown the place was. I was expecting to see tree-lined streets and Clark Gable, but instead I just saw boarded-up buildings and tourists from Iowa.

I stopped in front of Frederick's of Hollywood, the lingerie store, to watch girls walk in and out. They were all wearing tiny shorts and high heels and they were super hot. I couldn't get over how beautiful their bodies were—it was as though they had been manufactured somewhere. Oh . . . duh! I followed these girls around for a few blocks, staring at them. Then some mid-thirties surfer dude on a skateboard hit me in the back of my head and said, "What are you looking at, punk?" I got freaked out and went in the other direction. I didn't understand why he was so aggressive and angry, or why a guy in his mid-thirties was on a skateboard.

After a week of spooning with Anders and Olaf, I was ready to move on. I packed up all my stuff, got on a bus, and asked the driver, "I'd like to live in Hollywood. Can you take me there?"

"We're already in Hollywood," he said.

"Right," I said. "But I can't exactly live on Hollywood Boulevard. Is there, like, a residential area of Hollywood?"

He said, "Well, I'm going to North Hollywood. How does that sound?"

"Is that still Hollywood?" I asked.

"Sure," he said.

"Cool," I said. "Take me there."

North Hollywood turned out to be in the San Fernando Valley, seven miles away from the center of Hollywood. But even after the bus dropped me off there, I had no clue. I walked a block, rented an apartment, and settled in. It was a week before I realized that I wasn't really in Hollywood anymore, but I'd already signed a year-long lease.

During my first six months, I didn't exactly have laser focus in terms of my career. I just tried to fit into the Los Angeles culture and do all the things I thought Californians did. The thing is, all my knowledge of California came from TV shows, so I just did what TV characters did: I worked out, drank protein shakes, and went to the tanning salon three times a week. I even bought a tanning membership, if you can believe that. Despite the fact that I was all brown with these huge white marks around my eyes from the goggles, I thought I looked good. And the girl working there, who was as brown and leathery as a football, assured me that tanning was beneficial to my health. She said, "UVAs from the sun are pretty good. But UVAs from a machine are fantastic."

The other thing I did a lot was vacuum. This was my first time living away from home—I was really excited to have my own place and my own rules, so I spent all my time taking care of my apartment. I painted walls, caulked toilets, and fixed holes in the ceiling. Then, as I was putting down the last piece of Astroturf on the outside patio, my next door neighbor shouted out, "What the hell are you doing?"

"I'm fixing up my place," I said, proudly.

"Dude, you live in a fucking rental," he said.

Just like that, the thrill of cleaning disappeared. Meanwhile, my money was running out. It was time to get my life together. I needed a job.

I walked up and down Ventura Boulevard for miles, from Vineland all the way past Coldwater Canyon, putting in at least fifty applications at different restaurants. I figured it would be pretty easy to get something. Sure, I had absolutely no skills or real experience, but it's not like I was looking for anything glamorous. I wanted to be a waiter. Even a busboy would do.

Unfortunately, the town was full of struggling actors and writers and musicians. Apparently, all of them were better qualified for life in the food service industry than I was. I had to pound the pavement even harder to get a job. Finally, after an initial interview and a series of intense callbacks, I got an offer. For the position of host, the lowest man on the totem pole, at Red Lobster. I accepted.

———

I had already worked at the Red Lobster in Philadelphia, when I was a junior in high school. After a few months, I got fired for being drunk. Actually, my mom had me fired. I had been hanging out with my friends all day, getting plastered. I was so hammered that I couldn't even find the bus stop. So instead of getting on a bus and going to work, I just stumbled home, said hi to my mom, then staggered up to bed. The next day my boss called. My mom picked up the phone. He said, "Is your son there? I need to talk to him."

"Why?" she said, "What's there to talk about?"

"I need to talk to Jamie about his absence."

"His absence?" she said, "How about his drunkenness?"

My boss was totally understanding, saying, "Well, I was young once. Boys will be boys."

My mom insisted, "You're not helping him by letting him miss work when he's drunk. You need to teach him a lesson. I mean, what if he becomes an airline pilot and flies drunk? You need to fire him!"

"Are you sure?" he said.

"Absolutely."

Can you believe that? Actually, I don't know why I'm even surprised. That's my mom—Justice Josie. When I was arrested for public urination a few months before, she wouldn't bail me out of jail until the next day. When she finally came to get me, she gave me a scowl and said, "Urine trouble."

My mom worked my boss into such a frenzy that when she put me on the phone, he just blurted out, "Jamie, you're fired. And get some help." Then he hung up on me.

Luckily, my dubious history with the east coast chapter of Red Lobster didn't prevent my being hired at the Ventura Boulevard branch. However, the California Red Lobster was a world of its own. One of my duties there was to take the garbage out after work. Whenever I emptied the trash at night, I saw this bum who hung out by the dumpster. I think he lived there. I felt bad for him, so one night I walked up to him with a bunch of bread I had taken from the restaurant.

"Hi, how are you doing?" I asked, offering him the bread. "Do you want some of this to eat?"

"Oh, no thank you," he said. "I don't eat starches."

"Why?

"Carbs make me bloated," he said. "But do you have any lobster tails or shrimp? Or maybe some scallops?"

"Sorry. I just have bread," I said.

He shook his head. I couldn't believe it. What, was this guy on Atkins?

———

Every Friday night, people would come to the restaurant and have to wait forty minutes for a table. Why anyone would choose to wait this long to eat at a Red Lobster is still beyond me. Anyway, they would be in a huge line, pissed off, taking their frustrations out on me. One time, this nice old man came to the head of the line in the middle of a crowded Friday night. "Okay," he announced, "I'm ready to be seated now."

"I'm sorry," I told him, "You're going to have to wait."

"What do you mean? I'm here. I'm ready now."

"Yes, I know that you are here and ready now," I said, calmly. "And all these other people are here and ready now too."

"How long is the wait?"

"About forty-five minutes."

"What?" he yelled. "This isn't Spago! Ten minutes or I'm leaving!"

"Well, you're probably going to have to leave," I informed him.

His face turned beet red and he screamed at the top of his lungs, "YOU PIMPLE FACE!"

This was the kind of abuse I got on a daily basis. It was enough to make you hate humans. I decided to get on the customers' good side by becoming more "California." I started dropping words like "bro" and "buddy" into sentences and putting my arm around people when they came into the restaurant. I thought they were enjoying it, until this one customer, Fred, started shouting at me, "Pleeeease! Do NOT touch me! You have a problem with boundaries!"

"Okay," I told him. *What are boundaries?* I wondered.

"NEVER AGAIN!" he screamed back.

God, he was so angry! Joan Rivers had never told me there'd be days like this.

———

The job blew. I mean, I was making $4.65 an hour and I got paid every two weeks. But it did have some advantages. Mainly, it provided me with some of my earliest brushes with fame. My first actual celebrity spotting in LA was an actor by the name of Robert Costanza who I recognized from Shredded Wheat commercials. I wanted to talk to him so badly, but I couldn't do it. I mean, how do you approach Jesus? My second spotting was Courtney Cox through the window, at Blockbuster Video. "OH MY GOD!" I screamed, pulling my friend into the store. "That's the chick from *Family Ties!*"

"Who?" he said. "OH MY GOD! She was also in that Springsteen video!"

I couldn't believe it. I mean, seriously, what was she doing there? She was famous! We stared at each other. Actually, I stared at her. She just looked at me, scared. I really wanted to ask her something, but I couldn't. I think I freaked her out. I kept shuffling over to her section, and she kept shuffling away. I felt like we made a connection. I'm sure that's what John Hinckley Jr. told himself too.

I thought these encounters were amazing. But they paled in comparison to my experience at the Red Lobster, where I worked among celebrities on a *daily basis*. That's right—my fellow employees were famous! One of my cohosts was the real sister of Lara Jill Miller, the middle sister on *Gimme a Break!* Although I tried to play it cool and hide my excitement, I couldn't help constantly turning to her at the host stand and blurting out, "I can't believe your sister was on *Gimme a Break!*"

"It's no big deal," she said. "I used to do commercials. So what?"

"I want to do commercials," I said.

"So get an agent," she said, as she turned to the customers. "Johnson? Party of four?"

I thought, *I'm rubbing elbows with the rich and famous!* The proximity made me feel like I was *this close* to becoming a star myself. Unfortunately, all the celebrity-sister talk made her kind of angry. But sometimes she indulged me. Once, she took me to her sister's house in the Valley. It was huge, with a big black-bottomed pool.

I was overwhelmed. This was massive culture shock for me. Before I came out to LA, I had never even seen a Mercedes, let alone ridden in one. When I finally did, I wouldn't touch anything for fear of scratching it. Now, here I was, in this enormous mansion. The whole time I was swimming I was thinking to myself, *I'm swimming in a black-bottomed pool at Lara Jill Miller's house! The middle sister on* Gimme a Break! I think there may have actually been some flirtation between Lara Jill's sister and me, but I was too impressed with the pool to notice it.

Another one of my cohosts was a celebrity sibling as well—the sister of David Faustino, Bud Bundy from *Married With Children*. I didn't realize who she was until Bud Bundy himself came into the restaurant. I walked him to his table, openly staring. "Hey Bud," I blurted, "You're on that TV show! You're great!"

He just smiled, said thanks, and sat down. This place was amazing, like a celebrity sibling shellfish soirée. Two celebrities, two sisters, too weird. I ran back to the stand, grabbed my coworker's shoulder, and blurted out, "I can not *believe* you're Bud Bundy's sister!"

"Yeah, whatever. It's no big deal. I've been on that show too."

I badgered her with questions about what Bud liked to do in his spare time and what it felt like to be famous. She just stared at me, and then went to seat a customer. She was pretty hot, by the way. She looked like Bud, but with huge tits.

I couldn't get over how blasé these celebrity siblings were. They were all LA kids who had grown up around movie stars and money and fame. They'd seen everything by the time they were twelve and were bored already. In my eyes, simply reading about famous people was exciting. Working with their siblings was even more thrilling. But actually being able to seat them? Well, that was fucking HUGE. Perched at the host desk at Red Lobster, I really felt like I was mingling with the movers and the shakers of Tinseltown.

Lara Jill Miller and David Faustino paled in comparison to my next encounter. One day, this guy came into the restaurant and asked for a table. I told him we had no seats, not really paying attention—I was busy staring at my seating chart trying to figure out who had an open station.

"No seats," he repeatedly calmly. "You don't have nothing for me. For *me*?"

Without bothering to look up from my seating chart, I repeated, "No. No seats."

"So you don't have anything available?" he persisted.

"Look, dude, I told you NO SEATS!" I shot back. He was really starting to get on my nerves. I looked up. It was Arsenio Hall.

"Oh my God. ARSENIO HALL! It's you!" I shrieked, like a five-year-old girl.

He looked dead at me and said, "Still no seats?"

I shrieked back, "NO! We still don't have any seats!"

"All right, cool," he said. "I'll be back."

This was at the height of Arsenio's TV show, when he was really large. I was so star struck that I didn't know what to do with myself. I felt a nervous energy run through my whole body.

I took Arsenio at his word, waiting patiently for him to return. I wanted to seat him so badly, but I didn't know how. I mean, who was I to handle this kind of a celebrity? Then, I thought that maybe if I impressed him, he'd help me launch my career. One Sunday, I got my wish and Arsenio walked back into the Lobster. I begged my cohost to let me walk him to his table and he agreed. I was so excited, thinking to myself, *I am going to make it* right now!

I walked him to the table, all the while trying to come up with a clever remark, something that would knock him off his feet. I noticed that Arsenio was wearing extremely thick Rayban sunglasses. I had my opening. "Hey, bro," I began, "you've got to get a new disguise. We *all* know it's you under those sunglasses!"

Whoo! Haha! I was on fire!

Arsenio cleared his throat. Then, he said, in a very serious tone, "I don't wear these sunglasses to hide who I am. I wear these sunglasses to protect me from the UVA rays."

"Why? They're good for you," I said.

"Look, man, I don't want the sun in my face, a'ight?"

We were in the darkest, most cramped section of the restaurant. It was pitch black outside. But I didn't want to say anything rude. Instead, I wanted to give him something that was simultaneously understanding and witty. I came up with saying, "Whoo Whoo Whoo!" while pumping my fist.

In a flash, Arsenio opened his menu . . . and closed my window of opportunity. I was disappointed, but I figured the upside was that the story would make a good anecdote on Arsenio's show after I was famous. Five years later, I tried out for standup on Arsenio's show and didn't qualify. So I guess there actually was no upside.

———

I really thought it was possible to get discovered at Red Lobster. My coworkers just discouraged me, until, finally, someone decided to lend a hand —an Asian bartender named Henry Cho.

Henry Cho was super-friendly. He was always walking around, going, "Hey! I'm Henry Cho!" Henry also had really screwed up teeth. I thought that because I had pimples, we kind of shared a common bond of ugliness.

One day, Henry shouted out from behind the bar, "Hey Jamie! I think I can help you with your acting!"

Everyone there knew that I wanted to be an actor, but no one had offered to help me before. I was thrilled. "*Really*?" I said.

"Yeah," he said.

"You mean you can get me an agent?" I asked, in utter disbelief.

"Well, sure, it kind of acts like an agent," Henry said.

"So is he like a real agent?" I asked. I was salivating at this point.

"What are you talking about?" he said.

"My acting? The acting you're gonna help me with?

"Nooooooo!" he smiled. "I said I could help you with your ACNE."

I was so disappointed. Henry continued, "Pour some lemon juice on it at night. The juice will act as a chemical AGENT and dry the ACNE right up!"

Who was I, Jan Brady? Was this my freckles episode?

"No thanks," I said. "I don't want your help."

"Whatever," he said, now angry.

"What makes you think you're so great anyway?" I asked him.

"Because I get it," he said.

"Get what?"

"Sex!" he said.

"What makes you think that I don't get sex?" I asked him.

"All that ACNE!" he said.

It was right then and there that I started to hate Henry Cho. I went back to the host stand and greeted customers, acne and all. Fuck it. My acne would eventually clear up, but he'd always be stuck with those god-awful teeth, the little bitch. (Note to readers: sometimes I might sound like I'm a little gay. I'm not gay—I'm just a baby. I whine a lot. But I'm not gay. Although if I were gay, I'd probably whine about that, too.)

———

Henry was right about one thing—my sex life left something to be desired. In fact, I didn't have sex at all. Surprisingly enough, no one wanted to sleep with a struggling actor/acne victim/restaurant host. Then, a light on the horizon.

Ginger was a thirty-nine-year-old waitress at Red Lobster. She had a Hell's Angels, been-through-the-mill, someone-rode-her-hard-and-put-her-away-wet vibe about her. Tough as nails and total trailer trash. I was behind the host stand, like always, taking names and finessing customers, when she snuck up behind me. "Hey baby," she purred into my left ear. "Take a sip of this."

She handed me a big Red Lobster glass filled with some sort of liquid. "What is it?" I asked.

"Just taste it."

I took a sip, thinking it was one of the Lobster's signature fruity drinks. "Oh my god!" I said. "There's alcohol in that! And I have a Red Lobster record!"

"I just added a little sneaky-peek of vodka to it."

"I don't really drink anymore," I told her.

She giggled. "Don't worry about it."

"But we could get in trouble. We could get fired."

"Like I give a shit." She looked me up and down, and then asked, "How old are you?"

"Nineteen."

She wound up, swatted my ass, grabbed it and held it. "Nice. Real nice for nineteen."

She walked away. I turned around to the desk, where a customer said, "Jesus Christ. If that wasn't an open invitation, I don't know what it was."

After work, Ginger handed me a note with her phone number. It read, "For a good time, call Ginger. I'll show you where the sun don't shine." The note also featured a little picture she'd drawn of a female stick figure bending over. I was so inexperienced that I actually showed the note to the Mexican busboys, trying to make sure of Ginger's intentions.

"Go for it, holmes," they said.

"Maybe I'm misinterpreting?" I asked.

"Let her misinterpret your deeeck," they said.

"But Jorge, what do you think she meant by it?" I asked.

"To get fucked."

"Really?"

"¡Sí!"

I called her the next day. She said, "Hey, I live down the street from you. Why don't you ride your little bike over here?"

I pedaled up to her apartment, which was dark and run-down. When I went inside, Ginger was smoking a joint. She offered me a hit.

"I don't get high," I said.

"Well, what do you want to do?" she asked, suddenly coy.

I shrugged my shoulders.

"You're so sweet," she said. "Tell me about yourself. What do you like to do for fun?"

I didn't know what to do. In one day, Ginger had gone from a bucking bronco to a little pony. What did she want from me? A sonnet? All of a sudden, I was overtaken by a massive amount of horniness, which somehow traveled from my pants to my mouth. I got serious.

"I didn't come here to smoke weed," I said. "And I didn't come here to talk. So if that's what you want, forget it. I think you know what I came here to do."

I just stood there, not believing what I'd just said. Or rather, what my penis had made me say.

Suddenly, she clenched her teeth angrily and said, "Okay you little fucker. Get in that bedroom right now." I walked in, a little scared. Then, Ginger came up from behind me, ripped off my clothes, pushed me down on the bed and climbed on top of me. She began to wrestle me into different positions, like she was Jake the Snake. She threw her hands in the air, let out a stream of profanities, and proceeded to make noises like a dying pterodactyl. It was the most intense sexual experience I'd ever had.

Take that, Henry Cho!

From Now On, You'll Be a Salesman Named Jim

During the Red Lobster era, I decided to get another job—working behind the desk at Nautilus Plus Gym from six A.M. to two P.M., Monday through Friday. The work was mind-numbing. I checked membership cards until about eight A.M. After that, I cleaned weights, organized jump ropes, and stacked aerobics steps.

I also trained gym members, but I was so incompetent that I still feel guilty calling myself a trainer. Basically, the gym had a circuit training program that lasted thirty minutes. I just followed people around as they did the program to make sure that they were going on the machines in the right order and staying on them for the full time. I actually had to spot them sometimes, which was a joke, because I had no idea what to do. In fact, I still have a scar on my chin from the time I dropped a weight on my face.

The gym was huge, like a factory. There were a bunch of guys just like me, doing the same job. We all looked exactly the same because we had to wear identical red shirts. This made it easy to blend into the background and sort of disappear. So instead of working, I took to hiding in different places in the gym and reading about celebrities from the magazines that gymgoers would leave behind. I remember going into the steam room with someone's *People* magazine and seeing an article about Julia Roberts, right after *Pretty Woman* came out. They were saying she was going to be Hollywood's brightest new star.

I read a book about Arnold Schwarzenegger, where he said that if you could conquer your body, you could conquer the world. Muscles equaled success. So I really believed that if I got big and buff, good things would start happening for me. In an effort to bulk up, I brought a huge tub of spaghetti to the gym every day. My favorite thing to do was make a big bed of toilet paper rolls in the stock room, and hide there, just hanging out and eating spaghetti. The guy who trained me had told me that the stock room was *the* place to hide out from the bosses. When I first got there, I found six other guys doing the same thing, minus the spaghetti and the *People* magazine.

I also used to close up the gym every once in a while. When I was the only person in the place, I would walk onto the aerobics stage and pretend to do standup comedy to a crowd that wasn't there. My jokes were all cheesy and clichéd, which wasn't really a surprise, since the very fact that I was doing standup to an empty room was, in and of itself, cheesy and clichéd.

The gym wasn't as good as Red Lobster in terms of celebrity sightings, except for Paul Reiser, who used to work out with a German trainer. Paul always had a smug look on his face. This was during the prime of his show, *My Two Dads*, so he must have been pumped. Though he came in a lot, we only had one semi-interaction, when he came up to the desk to sign in. I was sitting behind it, listening to a walkman, with the volume turned down. He pointed to my walkman, and then said to his German trainer, "You know the great thing about those things is that this asshole can't hear what I'm saying."

I turned to him and said, "What's that?"

His face went white. "Oh, nothing. Nothing at all." He was totally freaked out. He never looked at me again, which I didn't mind.

While my time at Red Lobster was spent angering the customers, here I was more focused on pissing off my fellow Nautilus Plus employees. Somehow, I accidentally turned them into my enemies, one by one. First, there was an incident with a trainer. We were hiding in the stockroom, eating spaghetti, when he asked me, "What do you think of that new girl?"

"Who?" I asked, "Rambo?" She was a really big girl, who looked kind of like an Amazon. She had a face like a hamburger and she was super-muscular, to the point of dudeishness.

"Yeah," he said.

"I don't know," I said. "She's kind of a she-male. Why are you asking me?"

"Because I've been dating her."

Oops. I had only one opportunity to make this all better and say the right thing. "What's her ass like?" I asked.

He screamed, "None of your business!" Then he left me alone in the stockroom with my spaghetti. I sat there, eating and reading about how Bill Cosby was now making a million dollars a week.

The same trainer was also an aspiring actor. He knew that I wanted to act, so he gave me some advice, telling me to get headshots. He even gave me the number of a photographer who could shoot them for me, then said, "Call me after you get them and I'll help you pick out the best ones." A headshot, by the way, is just what it sounds like—a picture of your head. It's what all actors use in order to identify themselves, so the person casting them can have a visual reference before they meet the person. On the back is a résumé filled with lies.

After I got the headshots, I called him up. He said I could go over to his house at two-thirty that day, and we would go through the pictures together. He was really nice and very helpful.

So I rode my bike over to his apartment and rang the buzzer. There was no answer. I buzzed three more times, until someone walked out of the building. I caught the door and went in. I walked up to his apartment and knocked a few times. No response. The door was open, so I just pushed it gently and stepped inside. I called out, "Hello? Craig? Hello?"

No one answered. I sat down on his couch and continued to wait. All of a sudden, he came out in a towel, screaming, "Hey, get the fuck out of here! How'd you get in here? Get the fuck out!"

"But I have my headshots," I stammered.

"Get out!" he yelled.

"But you said you would help me."

"Get the fuck out," he said. "If someone doesn't answer the door, that means they're not home."

"But I knew you were home," I said.

"Well, what if I was up here jerking off? Huh? Huh? You just don't walk in on somebody. I'm not home. If I don't answer, then I'm not home! YOU'RE TRESPASSING, YOU FUCKING RUNT!"

So I left. I had never seen somebody change so quickly. I don't know what happened. I think he was bipolar. Maybe he was in the bathroom with Rambo. I was really upset, especially because I thought having a good résumé and headshot would be my golden goose.

Eventually, I took it to the top at Nautilus Plus and pissed off my boss. One day, when I was hiding out and eating my pasta, he called me into his office and sat me down for a heart to heart.

"Jim," he started.

"Um, my name is Jamie," I said.

"Jamie is a girl's name," he said. "From now on, you're Jim."

"Okay."

"Jim, you've been working here as a clean-up guy slash counter guy long enough. It's time for you to either move up or move out. We want to talk to you about becoming a salesman."

I couldn't believe these guys were thinking about making me a salesman. They had absolutely no reason to promote me. I mean, I didn't do anything. I sat at the front desk and ate pasta. I guess my boss thought I fit the profile.

He could see that I wasn't too excited about the opportunity, because he continued the hard sell. This was before *Glengarry Glen Ross* came out, but I swear, his tone was exactly the same as in Alec Baldwin's big speech.

"Jim," he started, "I don't know if you know anything about me, but I make sixty-three thousand dollars a year. I have a Porsche and a house and I started in your job."

"That's cool," I said. "How long did it take you?"

"Eight years, Jim. Eight years to make sixty-three thousand dollars a year," he boasted.

"Well, that's pretty good," I said.

"Pretty good, pal? What do you make? Four twenty-five an hour?"

"Well, actually, I'd like a raise," I said.

He just stared as me, as I continued.

"Besides, sixty-three thousand dollars isn't that much," I said. "You could be on a series and make that in two weeks. In fact, Julia Roberts is going to make triple her last salary due to the success of *Pretty Woman*, although she has said that she will not do a sequel."

He stared at me like I was a guy who rode a dirty ten-speed bike to work, which I was. "Jim, you know what your chances of getting on one of these television shows are? About a million to one, buddy. All right? Now, do you want to sit here and shine weights for the rest of your life, or do you want to try to make sixty-three thousand dollars a year?"

I took a bite of spaghetti. I knew that if I said yes, I was going to end up one of those tools wearing hair gel and a pinky ring, pushing gym memberships on MILFs and husband hunters with lopsided breast implants. It would be soul-sucking.

I must have paused too long. My boss shook his head. "I'm not getting a lot of enthusiasm out of you, Jim. You don't understand the whole Nautilus spirit we got here. I think it's time for you to go."

So in one conversation, I went from being promoted to being fired. It wasn't the first time—and it certainly wouldn't be the last.

Just Follow The Bouncing Ball

My apartment complex in North Hollywood was becoming the Melrose Place of the Valley. It was filled with total miscreants, in the best possible sense. It was a mix of musicians, bank workers, hippies, trailer trash, fat chicks, homeboys, immigrants, former jocks, and porno actresses. Most people wanted to do something different with their lives, but they were too busy taking E and petting each other's faces to do anything about it. It was a wonderful little building where everyone knew each other's business, and people left their doors open. I became friends with everyone except the porn stars, who wanted nothing to do with me.

My next door neighbor and I had a side business, grooming the trailer trash man who lived downstairs. Trailer Trash Guy knew we were broke and tried to help us out by letting us shave his beard for money. We would take an electric razor, each shave one side of his face, and then apply aftershave. He paid us ten bucks per side. It sounds a little weird, but it was totally innocent . . . I think. Afterward, we would go to Little Caesar's Pizza and get two pies for $9.99.

It was a great situation. Then, new owners bought the building and raised the rent substantially. So I moved to the cheapest place I could find, which was still more than I'd been paying. The new building was like a nursing home. It was dark and gloomy—a shithole for geriatrics. The woman who ran the place seemed like she'd lived there for a hundred and seventy years, and was constantly looking for ways to get rid of me. I had all these cockroaches in my apartment. I'm not talking regular cockroaches. These had wings and they flew. *They* should have paid rent.

"Can't you get rid of these things?" I asked the woman.

"No, they're Palominos," she said.

"So?"

"They're rare. That would be illegal."

Everybody who lived in this building was ancient. My neighbors were Lloyd, who sat on his toilet with both the bathroom and front doors open, and Jay, an x-ray technician who liked to brag about all the famous people he'd x-rayed. "I once gave Liz Taylor a barium enema," he said. "Her large intestine was absolutely perfect."

I had no friends except for these old people. It was really lonely. My neighbors were great to talk to in terms of humorous material, but it's not like they could really understand what I was going through or share any of it with me. I mean, I was twenty and they were on Medicare. I would tell them how depressed I was, and they would come back with, "You're depressed? My life's over." I mean, what was I going to say back to that? "Well . . . I can't get a commercial agent!"

Meanwhile, my cash flow was dwindling. I started cutting expenses. The first thing to go was my tanning membership. I was bummed. To compensate, I stole beta-carotene pills from the supplement store around the corner. They were supposed to make you tan, but they ended up turning my face and palms bright orange. Even then, money was tight. I had to engage in a lot of "eatlifting"—walking into supermarkets, eating muffins from the display case, then leaving. I figured they couldn't catch me because the food was in my body.

I started looking for a third job to supplement my income. I found a listing for *Tamara*, an interactive play, in the back pages of *Dramalogue*, a newspaper for actors. It had job listings, auditions for student films, ads for headshot photographers, and acting classes—everything. *Tamara* was a murder mystery set in a big Hollywood mansion. The audience followed the characters from room to room to witness scenes, but wasn't allowed to interact with the actors. Acting in this would have been a huge break, except I wasn't an actor—I was a waiter. I set up the bar and the meat and cheese platters, and I poured drinks during intermission. The only cool thing was that during the play, the actors would sometimes walk by my station and say, "Giuseppe! Vino?"

"Si," I'd answer. It made me feel like a real actor. But I was as far away from being a real actor as you could get. My week consisted of riding my bike to Red Lobster, stalking celebrities, hearing about my acne, caressing customers, then going home to sleep. On Wednesdays and Saturdays, I added some variety by taking two buses to *Tamara*. To make matters worse, people in LA thought taking the bus made you a spore. I spent hours sitting at bus stops and watching cars zoom by, their drivers glaring at me as if I were a wannabe actor with bad acne and no agent.

It was pretty dismal. I mean, I had come out here with these grand plans of becoming an extra. Bit by bit, I'd lowered my expectations to the point where, if I got an extra chicken finger at lunch, it was a good day.

Then, a lucky break. I got hit by a car!

I was riding my bike on a side street off of Ventura, when a rental car spun around the corner and clipped my back wheel. I flew off the bike and my ass hit the pavement—hard. My bike was totaled. The driver got out of his car, really freaked out. "Are you gonna sue?" he asked.

"Owwwww!" I screamed. I got up, grabbed my ass and hopped around the street, holding it like a chicken, if a chicken held its ass.

"Is that a yes?"

"I don't know dude, my ass is broken."

The next day I was bruised, but fine. I got a call from the rental car agency. "Are you going to sue?" they asked.

"I just want my bike fixed," I said.

"Fine. We'll cut you a check."

Two days later, I opened my mail to find a settlement agreement and a release form, promising that I wouldn't sue the rental car agency. I signed it, sent it back and got a check for $1500 the next week. Given this sudden cash influx, I decided to quit Red Lobster. I had enough money to just work at *Tamara* and concentrate on my acting for a little while.

During my year at *Tamara*, I tried hard to make contact with the other actors, but the only people who would talk to me were the waitresses, or as we called them, the wenches. The actors knew that I was just another wannabe aspiring to become what they already were. I knew it too, but it didn't stop me from trying. Once, when I was cleaning the bar, an actress in the play stopped near my station. She and our very gay, very affected prop man began discussing *Cinema Paradiso*, a film she had just seen.

The prop master asked, "Was it wonderful?"

"Darling," she said. "So fab I cannot tell you. Absolutely fab."

"Really? I'm aching to see it."

"Ohhhhhh, you must. It was so powerful. So fab."

While they both orgasmed on each other, I watched and waited for an opportunity to interject. I was very intimidated. I didn't even know what they were saying. It was the first time I'd heard someone use the word "fab." I was pretty proud of myself for figuring out that it meant fabulous.

They continued their conversation. "Ah," the prop guy said, "Were there subtitles?" He was hanging on her every syllable.

"Yes, of course. But I didn't need them. I speak fluent Italian."

I saw an opening, so I piped in. "Hey guys! Excuse me?" I said. "Subtitles? That means when there's writing at the bottom of the screen, right?"

She smirked and said, "Yes, darling. Ha ha ha. Just follow the bouncing ball." Then she and the prop man just laughed and laughed and laughed, as they walked away.

It kind of hurt my feelings. A year later I saw her in a Vagisil commercial. Now, every time I see Vagisil, I feel like it's laughing at me.

———

The crew at *Tamara* was made up of the kind of characters you can only meet in LA. Like Melissa, who used to save insects. Once, when I was about to pour a batch of old wine down an anthill, Melissa nearly killed herself diving on top of me, trying to stop the mass murder I was about to commit. Or Kiva, a really hot girl who used to be into soft porn and drugs, but had transformed herself into a Buddhist. Of course, I had to meet her after she was rehabilitated. Why can't I ever meet women like this when they're dejected and broken, in the middle of their tragic downward spiral? Story of my life.

Kiva was sweet. She tried to introduce me to Buddhism. In its most simplistic form, the Buddhist philosophy is that if you put good energy out into the world, good energy will be returned to you—basic karma. Kiva's friends were a bunch of actors who adapted the Buddhist philosophy to facilitate their acting careers. They got together once a week at someone's house to chant and request acting jobs from the universe. I guess they thought Buddha was the great casting director of the cosmos.

Kiva took me to a chanting session at one of her Buddhist friend's houses. I walked in and found eight people sitting in a circle, praying to a bowl of fruit. Actually, it was just an orange, a half-eaten banana and a couple of grapes. They sounded like a well-tuned monk engine, chanting "Nam-myoho-renge-kyo" over and over, but inserting some LA-isms in the middle, like, "Nam-myoho-renge-kyo-callback-for-I-will-get-a-callback-for-*One-Life-To-Live*-I-will-get-an-audition-for-*The-Single-Guy*-Nam-myoho-renge-kyo." I just wanted to chant for Kiva to take a shower with me.

Another guy who worked with me behind the bar was always trying to hook me up with jobs. He was a thirty-one-year-old hippie surfer dude from Orange County who played the guitar and had a van. He was constantly stoned. Stereotype, much?

One night he asked me, "Yo, dude, do you want to make some extra greenery?"

"What's that?"

"Cash."

"Yeah!" I said.

"Why don't you play Santa with me this year, bro," he said. "Santa's the gig, man. I do it every year. Take pictures with the kids. They cry. It's awesome."

He leaned in closer to me, as if he were sharing some amazing secret. He said, "And you know what, dude? If you do good on the Santa gig, just wait 'til Easter. The bunny equals money. You feel me?"

"I don't know," I said. "I'm not really good with kids. Plus I'm not fat."

"It's a cakewalk! A few ho-ho-hos and you're Audi 5000."

I took the gig. A week later I was surrounded by a group of kids, all of them screaming, "Santa! Santa! Santa!" and peeing on my leg. Good for my wallet, bad for my pants. They kept reciting these huge lists of presents they wanted. I said yes to everything as their parents glared at me. The whole time I kept thinking, "Do these kids realize that Santa just stole baked goods from Ralph's?"

Whenever Surfer Dude was too stoned to deal, he'd give me his other jobs. Once, I had to be Bart Simpson at an afternoon birthday party in the hood of East LA. I got there and was like, "Hey kids. It's me, Bart Simpson. Cowabunga, dude! Don't have a cow, man!"

The kids got really solemn and serious. They stared me down. "You're not Bart Simpson," they said.

"Yes I am."

They started shouting at me, "You're not the real Bart Simpson! You're a guy with a fake Bart Simpson head!"

They started to punch and kick me. Before long, they were pelting me with M & Ms and apples. I couldn't see anything, because my Bart Simpson head was twisted around. Then, I tripped. Even after I went down, they kept attacking me, pushing me and punching my big Bart head.

The whole time the mother just sat there, watching these

kids pummel me. In between blows to my head, I shouted to her, "Hey, can you control these brats?"

"I didn't think they would be able to tell the difference," she said. "Wow."

"Can you please do something?" I begged.

"I can't do nothing," she said. "They *crazy*."

Not Eggy Enough

I finally saved up enough money for a car. What I really wanted was a California convertible, but all I could afford was this big, beat up, gold 1969 Cadillac El Dorado, with 122,000 miles on it. I decided to make it a convertible myself. I went to U-Haul and rented a chainsaw, then went to my friend's garage, where we proceeded to cut the entire roof off. I didn't have enough money to rent a sander, so I just left all the jagged edges exposed. If I had gotten into a fender-bender, it probably would have severed my head.

Possible dismemberment was only one of the many downsides to having a permanent convertible. When it rained, I had no way to close up the roof. So I just drove the car anyway, water soaking me and everything inside. I was like Jed Clampett. Also, having no roof made me defenseless against hurtling projectiles. One time, I cut this guy off and he started honking at me incessantly. I gave him the finger, not thinking anything of it. He tried to sideswipe me a few times, screaming, "You're dead, cabrón!" Then, he got the car really close to me. His mom, who was in the passenger seat, threw an open can of Pepsi at my head. It broke open on the windshield, barely missing my face. I tore out of there, Pepsi spraying everywhere.

Despite all the drawbacks, I was really excited about the car, because I could now find employment outside the confines of LA's bus routes. *Tamara* was about to end its run, so the timing was perfect. I opened up *Dramalogue* and saw an ad that read, "Want to perform and get paid? Why not do singing telegrams?" I went down to Santa Fe Springs to the singing telegram company's office to audition. The owner asked me to sing three songs: "Happy Birthday," "Happy Anniversary," and "We Hate To See You Leaving." After the second song, he said, "Stop, you're hired." I was so excited.

I got paid seventy-five bucks a telegram, plus tip, so if I did a few per week, I would make a couple hundred bucks. Sometimes I got as many as two a day. I sang everything, everywhere—from birthdays in Torrance to retirement parties in El Segundo. I'd constantly get lost in bad neighborhoods. Whenever I slowed down the Cadillac to see addresses, people looked at me like I was about to perform a drive-by shooting. Let me tell you, there's nothing more uncomfortable than pulling up to a stoop in East LA and asking, "Pardon me, homeys, but is this 528 or 526? The number's blurred."

One time, I drove all the way down to Huntington Beach to sing at a bachelorette party—I was dressed like Jerry Lewis, complete with taped glasses and buck teeth. It was called a nerd-o-gram. I finished singing, all sweaty and tired, and asked the girl in charge for my money. She took me aside and said, "You know this is a strip-o-gram, right?"

"WHAT?" I said.

"Yeah," she said. "A strip-o-gram."

"No way," I said. "This is a nerd-o-gram. My boss must have made a mistake."

"No, it's a nerd-o-gram with a sexy strip."

"But I don't do sexy strip-o-grams," I said.

She smirked and said, "You do if you want to get paid."

I was totally broke and had driven all the way down there, so I really had no choice. I walked back into her living room and started dancing around. The crowd shouted, "Take it off!" I did. I had on my dirtiest pair of underwear—they were, like, ten-year-old Fruit of the Looms. "Naked! Naked!" they chanted. I stopped, pulled down my pants and mooned everyone, showing off my white ass. "Ewwwww," said the bachelorette.

When I was done, the girl in charge gave me my check and said, "You're not getting a tip." I had no cash, it was midnight, I was fifty miles from home. I started driving home and my car ran out of gas. I walked to a gas station and pleaded with the owner, promising to send him a check. Eventually, he gave me one dollar's worth of gas.

Fifteen minutes later, as I was driving through downtown Hollywood, my car started overheating and billowing black smoke. Then it caught on fire. It was hopeless. The engine was just done. I jumped out, took off the license plates and started hitchhiking. At about three A.M., some guy picked me up and drove me home. I never went back to retrieve the car—and now I had to take the bus to my telegram jobs.

———

Then, I got a break. I was in the singing telegram office, when the owner, Dickie, asked me, "Hey, do you want to be a California fresh egg?" Now, at this time, the California fresh eggs were getting huge. The egg had taken a lot of beating in the past for having too much cholesterol, but a study had just come out that claimed eggs were healthy, so they were making a comeback. So California was starting to promote the shit out of eggs.

This was right on the heels of the California Dancing Raisin Campaign, which featured a bunch of Claymation raisins dancing to "I Heard It Through the Grapevine." I don't know if anyone remembers this now, but at the time, they were the

Elvises of Claymation fruit. California wanted to do the same kind of marketing with these eggs. They were looking for actors to play the dancing eggs. If I got the job, the rest of the eggs and I would come out at the seventh inning of Padres games and the San Diego Chicken would pretend that he was laying us. We would get three hundred bucks a game. Also, we would get to perform at special events where they needed the California Fresh Eggs to dance.

I thought this could be a huge opportunity. I would get a credit for my résumé and national exposure. So I went in to meet the casting guy.

He said, "Name?"

"EGGbert!" I said, trying to impress him with my Grade A humor. An awkward pause. "Just kidding, it's Jamie!"

He said, "Turn to the left. Now turn to the right . . ."

I did.

"How tall are you?"

"Six feet."

"Okay," he said. "Thanks."

"But don't you want to see me dance?" I asked. I had worked out a whole break-dancing egg thing and also thrown in a little soft shoe.

"Nope," he said, very curt. "That will be all."

I left, completely frustrated. I hadn't even gotten a shot. Where had I gone wrong? Two days later, I found out that I didn't get the job. I asked Dickie, "What happened?"

He said, "The guy thought you weren't eggy enough."

I was crushed. I thought to myself, "What do I have to do to make it in this town?" This town being Santa Fe Springs.

July 8, 1989

I'm a freak when it comes to girls. I'm
so shy. When I catch eyes with them it
scares the shit out of me. It's painful.
I don't know what to say, I get all
tongue-tied. When I finally do get the
nerve to talk it comes out all psycho.
"Hey your pretty, can I smell you?"
I hate it.

4.

Funny Times in the 818

Acting is standing up naked and turning
around very slowly.
—Rosalind Russell

Good Dracula Impression, Bro

The Zanyside Theater was a dingy, hole-in-the-wall, thirty-seat theater, just down the street from my house. I passed it every day on my way to work. One morning, I spotted a sign in its window that read, "Improv Group Auditions." I thought that studying improv might be a good way to start my career, so I went in and met the instructor. He told me to come back and audition on Tuesday night. I was really excited, thinking, *This is how Mike Myers started out. This could lead to* Saturday Night Live*!*

I came back on Tuesday for the audition. I played acting games and did a couple of weird voices and a Scooby Doo impression. Then the instructor said, "You're in."

"No way!" I said, thrilled.

"Yes," he continued. "And the first thing I need from you is a hundred bucks."

"Why?" I asked.

"Dues." I had no clue what dues were. He said it was for the upkeep of the theater. I figured that it was the same as paying for an acting class. I dipped into my rent money and showed up to my first rehearsal on Thursday.

The first thing I noticed was how cliquey the group was. When we needed volunteers for improv games, I would raise my hand and no one would ever pick me to join in. And when they did, they were mean. The rudest person there was a guy named Guy. Guy was a dentist by day and comedian by night. He thought he was the next coming of Seinfeld. I thought he was a fucking dentist. For some reason, Guy had it out for me from the start. In order to improv a scene, we would have to create a situation. The teacher would say, "I need a physical description."

Guy would stare at my acne, laugh, and shout out, "Pimples!" In the next game, we'd yell out locations. Guy would look at me again and blurt out, "Dermatologist's office!" Then, he'd laugh hysterically.

One Saturday night, after two weeks of rehearsals, I actually got to do a show. It started at ten-thirty. For the first hour and a half, no one would let me perform. Finally, someone let me be in a sketch around midnight. I came out onstage as Dracula and said, literally, "Boo." I actually got a pretty good laugh, although there were only about four people in the audience. My classmates looked at me with mild respect, but by that point I was over it.

After the show, my friend came up to me and tried to be supportive, saying, "Good Dracula impression, bro." Then, Guy tried to get all buddy buddy with me, "Good line, dude. Hey, check out my headshot." He handed it over. It was one of those horrible one sheets, with him in, like, three different positions—one as a cop, being menacing, one as a teacher waving his finger, one with a beanie on his head. I fucking hated this guy Guy.

After that night, I knew Zanyside was a dead end, so I started looking around for a different improv group. Second City was the best, but they were closing their LA stage. The Groundlings were great, but I didn't have the money to join, and I heard that I would have to wait two years to get stage time. At that point, I didn't even know if I could act or anything. I needed to get onstage in front of an audience made up of actual people, to see if I had any semblance of talent. And "boo" wasn't enough of a challenge.

I picked up a *Dramalogue*, scouring the whole paper. Finally, I noticed a section called "Open Mic" that I had never seen or heard of before. An open mic night was held at a club— anyone could sign up to go onstage and do anything they wanted, sing or dance or tell jokes. That week's *Dramalogue* was advertising an open mic contest at a Howard Johnson's in the Valley. I had never thought about doing standup comedy before, but it seemed like a good way to see if I had any onstage talent. Besides, it was free and I only needed ten minutes of material. I figured it was worth a shot.

The only problem was that I had no act. To come up with some material, I asked my friend to tell me any jokes he knew. I came up with a few impressions of my neighbors and other random stories from my life. Finally, I watched a tape of a Dana Carvey special and stole his Bush impression. That was my ten minutes.

I wrote everything down on a little scrap of paper, hopped in a car with my friend and went to the Howard Johnson's to sign up. It was nothing special, just a little restaurant with a stage, but there were a lot of people in the crowd. There were a bunch of performers, mostly singers. A few dancers and comedians mixed in. Then, the MC called my name. I went up to the stage and rattled off the first joke from my piece of paper. I put my hands straight up over my head and asked, "What am I?"

The audience didn't say anything.

"I'm a fork!" I said. The joke got NO LAUGHS. Then, I commented on the joke bombing, "Oh, you don't know what a fork is? Is this the Ethiopian Howard Johnson's?" The audience laughed louder at that than at the joke itself. I went on. Some jokes sat there, flat like pancakes. Others killed. It was a very up and down set. But when I left the stage, they applauded pretty loudly. I thought to myself, *Hey, this isn't so bad.*

Then they announced the winners. I got second place. I couldn't believe it. My prize was a bottle of champagne, which wasn't as good as cash or anything—but still, it was something. And my friend was impressed. I was ecstatic. The way I saw it, it was May of 1990, I hadn't been out here a year yet, and already I was an award-winning comedian. On the way home, we passed the Zanyside Theater. I saw Guy on the sidewalk, telling jokes. "Hey, what do blondes call legwarmers? Earmuffs!"

He saw me in the car and waved. I gave him the finger. "Screw you," I said. "I'm a professional comic now."

I thought I'd do some open mic nights, make my way to big places like The Improvisation and eventually get my own sitcom. I figured that I wouldn't have to be on the open mic circuit for too long.

Little did I know that I would be on it for the next five years.

No Money in Improv

After placing second in my first competition ever, I thought the open mic circuit was going to be a cakewalk. Nothing could have been farther from the truth. I started doing standup regularly that summer at any place that had an open mic. I had about two or three gigs at a Motel Six in Calabasas, deep in the heart of the Valley, where I bombed. I entered a talent competition at a bowling alley in Reseda. I didn't even place. Then, I performed at Tony Roma's Rib House for a plate of ribs. Bombed again.

Audiences hated me.

It was torture. I was scared out of my mind. I couldn't even look at the crowd now. Eye contact would throw me. Not getting any laughs was so painful that I started to doubt myself and think that maybe I wasn't funny. After the summer was over, I said to myself, "I can't do this anymore." So I decided to quit—I'd find another way in.

I went back to improv and found another audition for a new group right away. The group was run by a forty-something guy named Larry and his mother. The San Fernando Valley public school system was paying Larry to put this group together so that they could go around to elementary and high schools, warning kids about the dangers of drugs, premarital sex, and peer pressure, told in little vignettes—education through humor.

I went down and auditioned. Larry gave me a box of hats. He said, "Every time I throw you a different hat, I want you to become the character who you think would wear the hat." He threw me a sailor cap and I became gay. Larry and his mom laughed, whispered to each other, then turned to me and said, "Welcome to The Improvables! Rehearsal's every Tuesday and Thursday." I perked back up. I was actually going to be paid to perform—twenty-five dollars a show. I was already making more money than Bill Cosby when he was an MC. And I had my own shower!

It was fun, but the performances were few and far between. People weren't exactly rushing to see an improv

group at their high school. We played some big pep rallies
though. One time there were like, nine hundred kids—and we
killed. It was easy to get laughs; all I had to do was make farting sounds on stage. I was living my dream. Then, after two
months, the group folded because Larry and his mom had creative differences.

Back to the drawing board. I looked in the paper and
found another audition for a paid improv group in the Valley.
The group was run by this Chinese guy named Lee Chang, and
it was going to be called "Chang's American Improv." (Not to
be confused with "Chang's Chinese Improv.") I auditioned and
got in. We had two weeks of rehearsals, three times a week, and
one show. Then, Lee realized that there was, as he put it, "no
money in improv," so he folded the group.

I'm not sure how this came as a surprise to him. I mean,
who sees improv as a Fortune 500 business? When have you
ever heard, "I'm Maria Bartiromo and tonight on *Squawk Box*,
we talk with Lee Chang, owner of the world's most profitable
improv troupe! Lee, how did you go from playing an Italian
restaurant in the 818 area code to making a billion dollars in
sales? The world wants to know."

Dances with Clits

Without the improv group, I had no creative outlet whatsoever.
It was frustrating to just sit around and wait for something to
happen. I needed to do something to get closer to my goal. My
friend's sister, who was in town for Thanksgiving dinner, told
me, "You should do standup again. It would be good for you."

That was the last thing that I wanted to do. But I realized
that she was right. The fact that I absolutely despised standup
and was petrified of going back was all the more reason to do
it—it was like a necessary evil. If could conquer standup, I
could do anything.

I started at a club called La Cabaret, which was on Ventura Boulevard, down the street from the Red Lobster. They hosted a comedy competition called "Funniest Person in the Valley." A comedian named Ben Segal had won it the summer before and received a $10,000 prize. I thought having this title would be an amazing way to launch a comedy career—and the money was great. So I decided to make myself known at the club.

From six to eight every night, anybody who signed up at La Cabaret could get onstage in their lounge and do a ten minute act. This was great for about two days, until I realized that normal people don't go to comedy clubs at six o'clock— the entire audience was made up of other comics.

I knew I was going nowhere in the lounge. I needed to convince the manager to book me in the main room for a fifteen minute guest set. Because the manager was constantly drunk, you could sometimes persuade him to book you through pure bullshitting. Ben Segal told me, "He *loves* credits. Say you just opened for Seinfeld at the Cleveland Chuckle Hut and you'll be in."

I had an opening.

The manager was only available from two to four P.M. on Thursdays. I called three Thursdays in a row and couldn't get through. There was a constant busy signal. Then, Ben told me I needed a phone with automatic redial, because every comic in LA was calling this guy at the same time. I borrowed my neighbor's phone, brought it to my place, and sat on my couch hitting redial over and over, trying to get the phone to ring. Finally, after an hour of this, the manager picked up and put me on hold. I knew that he hung up on everyone automatically after four P.M., so I watched the clock obsessively, yelling, "Come on, come on!" into the phone. At three-fifty-six, he picked up.

"Who's this?" he asked.

"Hi!" I said, "My name is Jamie!"

"Is this Jamie Foxx?" he asked. "Why didn't you use the private line?"

"No, I'm Jamie Kennedy. I'm a comic," I said.

"I've never heard of you," he said.

"Well," I said, "that's because I was opening for Pee Wee Herman at the Minneapolis Yuck Yuck Barn."

"Oh, the Barn?" he said, impressed. "How is Pee Wee?"

"He's great," I said.

There was an awkward pause.

I gathered up my courage and said, "So I'd like to showcase at your club?"

"Oh sure, all right," he said. "Next Friday, say nine-thirty, fifteen minutes?"

It was that easy. I put together the tightest material I had, which came out to be about four minutes. I figured the other eleven I could improv with the audience. When I got onstage, I started with my "what popular movies could be transformed into good pornos" bit. *Kindergarten Cop* could be *Kindergarten Cock*. *Silence of the Lambs? Silence, It's My Dick*. And *Dances with Wolves* becomes *Dances with Clits*. The crowd HAAAAATED it. They started heckling me. I turned to a woman in the audience and said, "Come on, ma'am. You have a clit, right?" This did not go over so well.

The manager came up to me after and said, "You have no act, and what little you have is x-rated. I can't *believe* Pee Wee would let you open up for him."

I was out once again.

Hammer Ain't Chinese

I decided that the Valley was too mainstream for me. I was gritty. I was edgy. I needed to take my act to the streets. So I found a place where my ground-breaking humor was sure to be appreciated: a *black* comedy club.

I started at The Comedy Act Theater, which was on 43rd and Crenshaw in LA, right near South Central. I saw a lot of great comedians there—Jamie Foxx, D.L. Hughley, Martin Lawrence, Cedric the Entertainer, Robert Townsend. So, one Friday night, I went to sign up for five minutes on stage. I was the only white guy there.

The MC called my name and said, "Now don't get too excited, y'all, but we have a brother from another mother coming up here. Put them hands together for the comedy stylings of the lily-white Jamie Kennedy!"

I got up there and completely froze. I just stared out into the silent crowd and thought, *What am I doing here?* I had to say something before I tanked. So I did the only thing a white comic could do—I started to make fun of black people.

I began ranting about Arsenio Hall. I said, "Have you ever noticed that when Arsenio has a guest on, he always welcomes them with insane enthusiasm? But, what if he had a dignitary on the show? Like Pope John Paul? He'd be like, '. . . AND NOOOW . . . for a maaan . . . who is respected round the worrrld . . . He got Jesus on speed dial! And he also is infaaallible! Let's give it up for my man in the funny little hat: POPE. JOHN. PAUL. **THE FOURTH**. IS IN DA HOUSE.'"

Then, I did a joke about gangs, how they were getting so popular that they should have their own award show. ". . . And for the best drive by shooting with a scope, the winner is . . . Bitch, give me the goddamn envelope . . . Junebug! Damn brother, two years in a row. He do got aim."

The crowd loved it. I was this skinny little white kid giving them shit. It was such a novelty that they ate it up. I came offstage with mad kudos.

The next week, I went back to the club with a LOT more confidence. The cock of the walk. The MC gave me a high five and a beautiful intro, "He may be white but his humor is tight.

A funny brother, y'all. Knocked 'em on dey ass last week. Give it up for Jamie Kennedy."

I went onstage, feeling good. I did my Arsenio bit . . . AND I ATE IT. I got a little nervous, but stumbled onto my gang bit. Complete silence. It was painful.

I thought, *Okay, I'll try out a new bit. That'll get them.* The bit was basically, what would MC Hammer sound like if he were Chinese? I danced around the stage and sang, "Doo doo doo doo, doo doo, doo doo, can't chop dis."

Nobody laughed. I kept on going, "Break it down! Eggroll time!"

Some eighty-year-old woman in the crowd yelled out, "That ain't Hammer!"

"I know," I said. "It's Hammer if he were Chinese, ma'am."

"He ain't Chinese," she shouted back. "He's black, like the rest of us!"

The whole crowd burst into laughter, then started to heckle me. "Fucka eggroll!" "Chop suey my dick, bitch!"

I couldn't even speak, because they were shouting so loudly. I leaned into the microphone and said, "Good night." Then, I ran offstage, down the aisle, and out of the club.

As I was speeding away, I heard the MC say, "Keep it going for Jason Kennedy! That's right, Jason! Keep on running! Maybe yo ass'll run into something funny!"

June 11, 1990

I hate it when people find out
I'm a comic. They ask me the
stupidest questons. "Hey you're a comic?
Are ya funny? What Am I
supposed to say? "No I suck sir,
I couldn't make a farting baby
smile. Don't see my show." Who else
has to go thru that? "Hey your A
hair dresser? Are ya good?" No I
cut your hair like a lawn mower
all uneven and shit. Then I throw
Acid on your scalp."

5.

Schooled

> *Men are born ignorant, not stupid—they*
> *are made stupid by education.*
> —Bertrand Russell

It's All About the Hero Can

I had been in LA for almost a year at this point, and I didn't feel like I'd made any progress. It was time to find an agent. I bought a guide to representatives at Samuel French, a bookstore for actors, and sent out a mass mailing of over two hundred headshots to agents. Only two people wrote back, both to reject me. Then, I got a letter from the Alexis Jones School for Acting and Modeling, offering me a position in their twelve-week program. The cool thing was that Alexis Jones was both an acting school and a talent agency. They guaranteed that they would represent you and send you out for auditions after you completed their course of study. I jumped at the chance.

Their guarantee turned out to be horseshit. In fact, the whole school turned out to be horseshit. It was in a mall in Orange County. The woman who owned it had a daughter who'd done a Pepto Bismol commercial that was really big in the late 1980s. She was on *The Tonight Show* because of it. This woman would always say, "Yep, my baby hit the big time. She got a national campaign and a seat next to Johnny Carson. World renowned. Bismol, baby!"

Even as I signed the first check, I knew that I was making a huge mistake. I thought, *What the hell am I doing? I just gave my money to a woman who thinks the big time is being the Pepto Bismol girl!*

I quickly realized that my instincts were right—the place was a total gyp. It was a modeling school. We were instructed in posing with soda cans and pizza boxes for commercials. They taught the girls to take bites of Domino's Pizza and coo, telling them to "flirt with the pizza!" The guys learned how to swig soda and then laugh as if they were achieving inner peace. We made the Mentos actors look subtle.

The Alexis Jones philosophy stated that the product was the most important thing about the commercial, much more important than the actor. Commercials were all about selling. "Always favor the product over your own face," they would scream out, as we strutted down the makeshift catwalk. They acted as if it were Milan: "Work it, WORK IT, OWN IT! Show me the hero can, baby!" The teachers referred to the Pepsi can as the hero can, because it was the star of the shoot. Actually, not every single Pepsi can could be the hero can, because a single commercial shoot might use twenty different cans from fifty angles. The hero can was the can that got the final close up with all the sexy can sweat dripping off of it and glistening in the light. The hero can was supposed to be like a beacon of hope to the audience and their families—it could stave off disease, help rekindle marriages, and ward off crime. Not to mention, it had beaten out all the other cans. That alone was truly heroic. We actually had a retired hero can in class, but it was off-limits. At the end of the course, we made little tapes of ourselves with mini-auditions on them. Only then were we allowed to touch the hero can.

I knew things were really bad when one of the teachers talked about paying your dues, using Tom Cruise as an example. The teacher's name was Ken, which was so appropriate, because he looked like a Ken doll. Ken said, "In order to be like Tom Cruise, you have to pay your dues like Cruise. You know, he really went through a lot."

I had just finished reading a biography of Tom Cruise, which said that he had worked three months in New York as a janitor before getting his first job in *Endless Love*. Then he got *Taps*, *The Outsiders*, and *Risky Business*, and from there his career went crazy.

I raised my hand and said, "Ken, Tom Cruise really didn't pay that many dues."

"Are you kidding?" he asked. "Do you know how many Broadway and Off Broadway plays he did? He struggled for ten years."

"Ken," I said. "That means he would have started acting when he was eight. He was in *Taps* when he was eighteen. He was a janitor for three months."

"You gotta get your facts straight, buddy," he said. "You don't know what you're talking about. He was an Off Broadway actor for years!"

"No, he was an Off Broadway janitor for three months."

"You're wrong!" he screamed. "Wrong!" He just couldn't believe that I was questioning him.

A girl standing next to me on the runway, posing with a bag of Doritos, suddenly hit me. "I can't believe you're going against the teacher," she said. "You're going to burn your bridges in Hollywood!"

"Baby, we're in Orange County," I said.

After twelve weeks I graduated from the school. They sent me out on one audition and I never heard from them again. Actually, it wasn't even an audition. They just gave me an address where I could leave my picture in a box and if the box owners liked it, then maybe they would call me in.

Six hundred and fifty bucks down the toilet. I was an idiot.

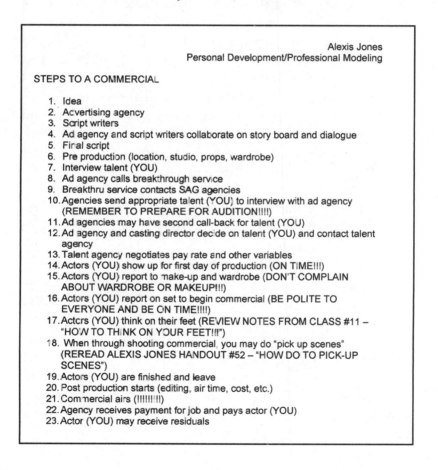

Alexis Jones
Personal Development/Professional Modeling

STEPS TO A COMMERCIAL

1. Idea
2. Advertising agency
3. Script writers
4. Ad agency and script writers collaborate on story board and dialogue
5. Final script
6. Pre production (location, studio, props, wardrobe)
7. Interview talent (YOU)
8. Ad agency calls breakthrough service
9. Breakthru service contacts SAG agencies
10. Agencies send appropriate talent (YOU) to interview with ad agency (REMEMBER TO PREPARE FOR AUDITION!!!!)
11. Ad agencies may have second call-back for talent (YOU)
12. Ad agency and casting director decide on talent (YOU) and contact talent agency
13. Talent agency negotiates pay rate and other variables
14. Actors (YOU) show up for first day of production (ON TIME!!!)
15. Actors (YOU) report to make-up and wardrobe (DON'T COMPLAIN ABOUT WARDROBE OR MAKEUP!!!)
16. Actors (YOU) report on set to begin commercial (BE POLITE TO EVERYONE AND BE ON TIME!!!!)
17. Actors (YOU) think on their feet (REVIEW NOTES FROM CLASS #11 – "HOW TO THINK ON YOUR FEET!!!")
18. When through shooting commercial, you may do "pick up scenes" (REREAD ALEXIS JONES HANDOUT #52 – "HOW DO TO PICK-UP SCENES")
19. Actors (YOU) are finished and leave
20. Post production starts (editing, air time, cost, etc.)
21. Commercial airs (!!!!!!!!!)
22. Agency receives payment for job and pays actor (YOU)
23. Actor (YOU) may receive residuals

The Errand Boy

I moved into a theater/acting school that I found through a newspaper ad. The woman who owned the place said that I could stay there for free in exchange for mopping the floors in the morning and emptying the trash at night. I had a little room in the attic above the theater with a bed, a desk, a phone, and a window that gave me roof access. My only companion was the caretaker of the theater, an old man who looked exactly like Robert Duvall when he played Boo Radley in *To Kill A Mockingbird*. Our friendship consisted of him constantly giving me dirty looks, then making turkey chili in his room and eating it with the door locked. I spent my days eating tuna, staring at Boo's door, and thinking of ways to make it big. Every night, I did the open mic circuit, bombing more often than not.

Through the open mic circuit, I met a four-hundred-pound comedian named Freddie "Fireplug" Fulsom. He was the big man on our campus, because he had been in the movie *Look Who's Talking Too*. He was twenty-one years old and played a fat sixth grader.

Freddie persuaded me to take acting classes again. He said, "Bro, you don't just wanna do comedy. You wanna be an actor too, well-rounded."

I kept thinking, *You're really well-rounded.*

I went to my first class with Freddie on a Saturday morning and it was all eight- and ten-year-olds—a bunch of kids! I wanted to get out of there, but Freddie thought that child classes were the way to go, because they were cheaper and we were still young enough to go out for younger roles. The teacher agreed with him. She said that we should start here, and if we did well, we could move up to the Tuesday night adult class. I decided that I might as well try it out for the day.

The first scene we did was from the TV show *Growing Pains*—material I could relate to. Everyone paired off and I was left alone. The teacher assigned me to partner up with this eight-year-old girl, Jessie.

We went off into a corner to rehearse our *Growing Pains* scene. It was one where the character "Boner" asks out Tracey Gold, who played Kirk Cameron's sister. The whole time we were working, Jessie's mom kept looking me up and down. She thought I was some sort of pervert because her daughter kept saying lines like, "Boner, you might be too much for me." When we finally went up on stage and "Boner" started to hit on Jessie, the rest of the kids went crazy, giggling like they had just heard the word "boobies" for the first time.

Despite the fact that most of my fellow students were still in single digits, this was the first acting workshop I had been to in LA where I felt like I could actually learn something. It was only eighty bucks a month and practical, too. We worked on useful things, like how to break down scripts for television, sitcoms, and one-hour dramas, since we were hoping for those kinds of auditions. In addition, I was kind of attracted to the teacher, Kelly, who was this earthy, sexy Southern woman. She had a very warm, maternal way of running the class. I decided to stay on.

Everything was going great. Then, the woman in charge of my theater home found out that I was taking Kelly's acting class. "You're an actor?" she asked. "You're supposed to be my janitor."

"I'm not an actor," I said.

Boo creeped around the corner and hissed, "He has sides from *Growing Pains* in his bedroom! I saw 'em."

I was caught. "I can do both," I said.

"No, actors are too flaky. You have to leave."

Fuck! I had only been there for two and a half months. I can't even begin to stress how long it felt at the time. When you're broke and desperate and starving, just getting up every day feels like climbing a mountain. Days passed like months and months like years.

I did the couch circuit for a few weeks. First, I stayed with an MC on the open mic circuit who dealt LSD tabs with Smurf faces on them. The MC was constantly on Gargamel and kept locking me out of the apartment. Then Freddie said, "Bro, you can't stay there. Sleep on my couch." It was fine for a week, but his shower was moldy. I know I sound like that bum from Red Lobster but it was really, *really* moldy. (Maybe I *am* gay.)

Then, I ran into Andy, one of my friends from the "The Improvables." Andy found out where I was staying and said, "Hey man, you can't be doing that! Come live with me. We can split the rent." His apartment was in Koreatown and cost only $180 a month. It was a godsend.

When I think about it now, I can't believe how many people took me under their wings at different points in my life. I'm not even sure that I realized how much of a favor Andy was doing me. Instead, I thought, *Christ, how come this guy can't come up with $180 a month on his own?* Then I moved in, and I couldn't even come up with $90 a month.

Because I now had to pay rent, I couldn't afford acting class anymore. I told my acting teacher Kelly about these financial problems, and she said, "You know what? I kind of need a little helper and assistant. Why don't you be my little apprentice, and then you can come to my class for free."

"Really? Okay," I said.

I started helping Kelly after class—organizing papers, getting scenes ready, sweeping up. Just basic stuff. Then I began running more personal errands, like picking up Kelly's flower bulbs and grocery shopping. She paid me a little bit of money and I was able to buy a used car—an old Ford Escort. Slowly, I started developing a crush on her. I would constantly be looking at her during class, over the sea of eight-year-olds, thinking about where I wanted to plant my own flower bulb.

Even on the first day of class, Kelly had seemed to be flirting with me, but I really didn't think anything of it. One, because I really was into my *Growing Pains* scene, and two, because who else was she going to flirt with? Freddie weighed four hundred pounds and all the other boys were eight.

After a month, my errand boy duties became even more personal. We were at Kelly's house on afternoon, cutting out dead roses from her rosebush and planting new bushes. When we finished, Kelly said, "I'm going to go take a bath while you rake these leaves."

"Sure," I said.

I began to rake. A few minutes later, Kelly called out, "Jamie, can you come here for a second?"

I went into the bathroom, and found her sitting in the tub, completely naked. There weren't even bubbles. I screamed, "WHOOOAAA!" and ran out. I was a total fag.

"What are you doing out there?" she asked, laughing.

"Raking your leaves," I said.

"Come on in," she said. "Don't be shy."

"I . . ."

"C'mon."

I walked back in. Her enormous breasts were just kind of floating there, nipples erect, like little soldiers saluting.

"Can you wash my back for me?" she asked.

I was really nervous, still not sure what was happening. I thought, *Is this like some weird sort of errand?* I grabbed the loofah with the longest plastic handle and started to do her back from outside the tub. (By the way, I know this sounds a lot like *Private Parts*, but it really happened.)

"Why don't you get in the tub and do that?" she asked. She smiled at me, waiting.

I managed to croak out, "Are you sure?"

"Yeah," Kelly said. "You're really dirty."

I took off my clothes and got into the tub. She grabbed me and slowly slid her tongue in my mouth. Boner wasn't just a *Growing Pains* character anymore.

After that, I got to graduate to the adult acting class.

6.

Won't You Take Me
to . . . Koreatown

> *If at first you don't succeed,*
> *failure may be your style.*
> —Quentin Crisp

Getting to Jeremy Land

When I was still in the children's acting class, an agent named Phyllis Weinberg came by one day, looking at little kids for possible representation. Phyllis, along with her partner, Blanche, owned a company called PBKA—Phyllis & Blanche's Kids Agency. She was an older Jewish lady who started out as an agent in New York, then came to LA to retire, but couldn't get the business out of her system. So she and Blanche opened up this agency, just for children. They represented them for commercials and bit parts in TV and film.

After class on Saturday, Phyllis scoped out the next Macaulay Culkin and schmoozed the prepubescent set, saying

"Honey! Call me!" Of course, all the stage mothers were up her ass, because they thought she held the keys to the kingdom. I wanted to be up her ass, too; I just didn't know how. She was a real agent with access to real auditions. She could be my savior.

I approached Kelly and asked, "Do you think Phyllis would meet me?"

"Maybe," she said. "She takes clients up to eighteen."

"But I'm twenty-one," I told her.

"But you play fifteen."

So I approached Phyllis and said, "Hi, my name is Jamie Kennedy. I'd like to know if I could come in and do a scene for you. Please?" Kelly vouched for me. Phyllis looked me up and down, then relented. She didn't know *what* to make of me.

I went to Phyllis's office for an audition. Their agency was on Ventura Boulevard, in the Valley, which might as well be in Guam, as far as anyone in the entertainment industry is concerned. Of course, I didn't know that at the time. Once I got there, Phyllis handed me a piece of paper, saying, "Okay, honey, I want you to read this scene."

I read it to myself.

"Okay," she said. "You ready?"

I nodded to my head, then cleared my throat and recited my line. "Hi. Welcome to Taco Bell. May I take your order?"

Phyllis said, "Hmmm. Yeah, um, break it up a bit. Like, 'HI, Welcome to Taco BELL!' Really stress the 'bell,' honey. Ring it."

I did it again. She said, "Yeah, um . . . have more fun with it."

"HEYYY!" I said, "WELCOME to Taco BELL! MAY I take YOUR order?"

"Take it down, sweetie. It's not summer stock."

After about ten tries she turned to her partner, Blanche, and said, "Whaddya think?"

Blanche said, "Hmmmmmmmmm . . ."

"He's tall," Phyllis said.

"Hmmmmmmmmm . . ."

"Okay," Phyllis said. "We'll take you."

Blanche said, "Yeah, what the hell."

Jackpot, baby! Phyllis said that I had to be available all the time for auditions, which made me even more excited. I just knew that all I needed was to get into a room. Then, I would be able to win people over.

Phyllis gave me a beeper and said, "When you see the code 911, it means that we've got a *national* commercial audition for you. Those are big, honey." This was in the days before everyone owned a cell phone, and having the pager was huge. For the first time, I felt like a real actor.

Phyllis and I had a strategy meeting, where she explained exactly how she was going to sell me. She said, "We think we can use you, but you're not exactly handsome. You're not ugly. But you're no John Stamos. You're just . . . off-beat. And that's where we plan to use you." She smiled, getting excited, then continued. "Do you know the boy with Down's Syndrome who's in the McDonald's commercials? The one where he worked the counter?" she asked.

"Yeah," I said.

"He's also off-beat."

"The retarded kid?" I asked.

"NO! Jeremy has Down's Syndrome!" she said. "He's just slow. He works all the time, though. Goes up against Corky from *Life Goes On*. He's our first actor in the off-beat category. We just had him. And now we have you."

"Seriously?" I asked.

Phyllis got huffy. "You have no idea how great Jeremy is in the room," she said. "If you could get to 'Jeremy Land,' you'd be golden, believe me. He just booked a Long John Silver commercial."

"Okay," I said.

"Good," Phyllis said. "Now, let's talk about your nose. Did you ever think of having it fixed?"

"No," I said.

"Because, you know, you could have it fixed."

"Why?"

"It's fat."

"No. I like my nose."

"Fine," she sniffed. "Be a big-nosed actor."

I thought, *This woman represents a mongoloid, and my nose isn't good enough for her.*

————

Phyllis started sending me out for every commercial. And I mean *every* commercial. Every delivery guy, pizza guy, teller guy, anything. Anything with a hat and a nametag. It was awesome!

I'd come home every day, play my messages and hear Phyllis's high-pitched voice, chirping, "Beep! Hello Jamie. This is your agent Phyllis calling. You have an audition tomorrow at nine-thirty A.M. It's for McDonald's, and it's a national commercial. You're going in for the role of counter boy. If you had a hat or a nametag, that would be very appropriate."

I'd push the button again, and it would be Phyllis, talking faster and faster. "Beep! Hello, Jamie. This is your agent Phyllis calling. You have an audition tomorrow at ten-fifteen A.M. It's for Burger King, and it's a national commercial. You're going in for the role of counter boy. If you had a hat or a name tag, that would be very appropriate."

Push the button. Phyllis—warp speed. "Beep! HelloJamie. ThisisyouragentPhylliscalling. Youhaveanauditiontomorrowat elevenfortyfiveam. It'sforKentuckyFriedChicken—"

It was really exciting at first, especially with the bigger auditions. My beeper would go off, and I would have to run to the Winchell's Donuts on Vine Street to use their payphone. Phyllis would say, "Kellogg's needs to see you *right now*. They're looking for a new spokesperson for Rice Krispies. Go snap, crackle, and pop for them honey! Knock 'em dead!" The urgency in her voice was great. It made me feel legitimate.

At first, I loved everything about auditioning. It was like buying a lottery ticket and scratching it. Nothing could get me down. I remember being on the phone at Winchell's one time, looking out through the window. There was a bum taking a shit on the sidewalk and eating an éclair at the same time. It was gross, but I didn't care because I had just gotten a callback for a Carl's Junior regional spot.

The thing is, I wasn't booking. Anything. Commercials were all about having the right look and being the right type— and I didn't fit in their box. I thought maybe I could do better in TV and film. Every time I asked Phyllis about it, she would say, "Honey, you have to get your feet wet. You're green!"

She had a point, but it's not like I was getting a ton of high-end auditions. I was really dealing with the dregs of Hollywood here. In one instance, I went to the office of a guy named Fritty Granada, who was producing a Spanish infomercial. Fritty had plastered his walls with pictures of himself with famous people. They were like his calling cards. In some of the photographs he was standing next to a celebrity, but the celebrity looked really uncomfortable, like, "Who the hell is this guy taking a picture with me?" And in some instances, it looked like the celebrity had no idea that their picture was even being taken.

The audition basically involved listening to him talk. "Yes, we have many commercials here in production in studios," he said. "We are planning to do many types of films." I nodded. "This is a small office, but very powerful," he continued. "Do not be put off by the furniture." I nodded again. "Right now I'm producing a TV show, you know. On Channel 43, you know, cable access. I mean, right now, the picture comes in a little fuzzy, but it's going to be a very good show."

In the middle of discussing his company's future, he stopped to get up and point at the famous people in the pictures. Then, he quizzed me. "Who's dis?" he asked.

"Clint Eastwood?"

"Yes! Who's dis?"

"Uh, Gene Hackman?"

"And who's dis?"

"Andy Garcia?"

"Andy Garcia," he repeated, finally satisfied. He pointed to each photograph in turn and said, "I work on film with him. I went to party with him. I know his mother."

After all that, I didn't get the job. The next audition I went on was for Chili's, to play the part of a Christmas elf. I sat outside, waiting with a wannabe Santa. He turned to me and said, "So, you're an actor? Did you study acting?"

I told him I had just finished a class. There was a long pause. "Well," Santa said, "You've got a long road ahead."

"Why is that?" I asked.

"It's just the beginning," Santa said. "You have a lot of disappointment to look forward to." I couldn't believe it—I'd finally met Santa, and he was a fucking asshole.

I went into Phyllis's office to have a talk.

"You know, Phyllis," I started. "I can do more than this commercial stuff. I'm studying to be an actor."

She'd probably heard this a hundred times from a hundred different actors, because she started to freak out and rant.

"Jamie!" she said, "How long have you been in the business? Four minutes? I've been in this business for thirty-five years. I have a three-year-old with more credits than you! If you're not in a national Huggies commercial by the time you're six, you should seriously consider getting out of this business."

"Phyllis, listen to me," I said. "I can do more than this. Robert De Niro, who's one of the greatest American actors of our day, didn't start acting until he was twenty-four or twenty-five."

"JAMIE!" she screamed at the top of her lungs, "ROBERT DE NIRO . . . IS NOT WITH THIS AGENCY!"

She took a deep breath and said, "I don't think I can help you anymore. You're just not ready." And that was the end of that. I had never booked a single commercial with Phyllis.

In the end, I went out on eighty-two commercial auditions before I booked my first one.

Jobs, Jobs, and More Jobs

I needed to find some way of supporting myself. Unfortunately, I was also the worst employee ever. For a few months, I got hired and fired once every two weeks. My first job was at Mrs. Gooch's Natural Food Store in Beverly Hills. I was a checkout clerk/grocery bagger, which seems pretty simple, but in fact required more preparation than anything else I'd done before. We had to train on the register for a week and then get tested on all the different codes for food. Fruits were particularly hard because there were so many, and if they were from another country, then it would affect the price code. It was all this useless information that I didn't want in my brain. Like, there would be navel oranges and Guatemalan navel oranges and seedless Guatemalan navel oranges grown organically, and all had different codes. And then there were the kiwis . . .

My coworkers weren't very open minded, which was sort of surprising considering that we were in an alternative, holistically-oriented environment. They were all about working at the supermarket and living the supermarket life. They all hung out together after work, dated fellow Gooches, and played on the Gooch softball team. They all gave me shit for not taking part in their Gooch games. My cobagger constantly made fun of me for trying to become an actor, saying "Fool, you don't even know the code for bok choy. How are you ever gonna memorize your lines?" He did have a point.

Mrs. Gooch's was an upscale store. A lot of rich people and celebrities shopped there. By this point, I'd started to get over my intimidation—just a function of being rejected so many times. Right after I started working, Meryl Streep came in. While I was bagging her groceries, I asked her how she got her agent. She mumbled something about Yale Drama School, grabbed her echinacea, and split. My fellow employees couldn't believe my nerve.

"What's wrong with you, dude? You don't talk to Meryl Streep," they said.

"What do you mean?"

"She's a living icon, man."

I didn't know that. I just watched TV. I never went to the movies. It's not like she was Arsenio Hall, who was on TV every night and had Magic Johnson for a best friend. *That* was a living icon.

A few days later, Luther Vandross came in. He walked over to my cash register with a bunch of sweet chard and asked me for a price. I sang, "That'll be $1.89," trying to sound like him. He frowned and walked away.

My boss called me into her office. "We have a problem," she said. "You're too chatty with the customers."

"What do you mean?"

"When celebrities come into the store, they don't want to be bothered," she said. "But you keep talking to them and asking them questions about how they made it."

"Who said that, Streep?"

"Yeah, for one."

"Come on, Meryl didn't care," I said.

"Yes she did."

She continued to list her grievances: "You make celebrities uncomfortable when you imitate them to their faces."

"I thought Luther liked it," I said.

"He didn't."

I promised that I would try to stop scaring the celebrities. A week later, Mindy Cohn, who played Natalie on *Facts of Life*, came into the store. I knew I wasn't supposed to talk to her, but I figured there was nothing wrong with being nice. Everyone liked compliments, even celebrities. So as I rang her up, I said, "*Facts of Life* was a good show. I really liked the episode where you guys went to Paris and Tootie got stuck at the Eiffel Tower."

"Thanks!" she chirped.

"What are you doing now?" I asked enthusiastically.

Her face fell.

"Nothing," she said, grimly. She seemed mad. Really mad.

I got fired. Next!

(By the way, I recently met Luther Vandross and told him how I got in trouble for singing to him at Mrs. Gooch's. He asked, "Oh, are you still working there?")

———

I got a job in Brentwood, at a place called Humphrey Yogurt. It wasn't exactly the perfect situation. The owners were cheap and didn't pay anything above minimum wage. My boss was a sophomore in high school named Tiffany, whose greatest pleasure was abusing me, her underling.

Every morning I would come in to hear my sixteen-year-old boss on the phone with one of her friends. "OMIGOD!" she'd say, "I cannot *believe* that you're even, like, *talking* to him!

After what he did? Okay, wait, hold on . . . I have someone here being insubordinate."

She'd turn to me, smirking, "Helloooooo, Mr. *Late*! You're like, soooo late! I have to write you up."

"Really? I'm only five minutes late."

"I so don't care," she'd say. "You were supposed to be here at, like, eight-thirty and it's, like, eight-thirty-five. You're *laaaaaate*. Oh, and put more sprinkles in the sprinkle holder. Oh, and we also need more crumbled peanut butter chips. Oh, and we need the Oreos to be chopped, not crushed." Then, she'd get back on the phone. "Ewwww, Simon?! Why? He'd better not be in our geometry class this year. I swear, I'll die. No, bye. Okay, bye. No, bye. Anyway, see you at Pom Pom! I will. No, I will. Bye."

I tried to ignore Tiffany. Then, one night, I made a fatal error. Tiffany told me she was going to some party. "Oh really," I said. "You're, like, allowed out? Isn't it, like, a school night?"

Tiffany flipped out, shouting, "Someone is not exercising good judgment! That's SO not the way to talk to your superior!"

"You're sixteen."

"Exactly," she said. "I'm sixteen and your boss. You're twenty-one and going nowhere. This is my summer job . . . and *your* career."

The next day, she got her final revenge. I was really hungry at work, and though we were only allowed to eat one tuna sandwich per shift, I ate two. Tiffany noticed. "You ate two sandwiches! Do you know what this means?"

It scared me.

"What?" I said.

"I have to write you up," she said.

"NO!"

"Um, yeah, your third one! You're so fourth period . . . HISTORY!"

And just like that, Tiffany got me fired. I think she was the maddest, richest girl I'd ever met. I mean, she lived in this huge house in Brentwood and drove a Jag—and yet she loathed *me*, living in a Koreatown shithole and driving a ten-year-old Ford Escort.

Next!

———

I found an ad in the paper for pages—the people who usher audience members in and out of television tapings at the various studios. The job was for the ABC show *Who's The Boss*, which starred Tony Danza as a nanny and Alyssa Milano as Tony's daughter. Basically, my job would be to lead people into the studio, wait for the taping to end, then lead people out. A taping could run up to three hours, during which time I would literally have nothing to do except sit in a chair, guard the door, and wait at my post.

I applied for the job, writing in my letter that "a page is not just an usher, but a liaison between star and fan. It is not a job to be taken lightly." At one of my three screening interviews, the personnel director told me that he really responded to the letter. However, he pointed out that I needed to remember that "being a page is a real job. It's important for real people to get to their seats on time at a screening of a real Hollywood show."

"Totally," I said, playing along. "I love getting people to their seats."

"You realize that as a page, you wouldn't actually be allowed to go back and talk to the actors," he said.

"Oh, no. Of course not."

"Remember," he said. "You are not allowed to leave your post."

At my first Friday night taping, I saw the actors come on stage. I immediately left my post to go watch them. As soon as

I got there, the other pages surrounded me and said, "What are you doing back here? This isn't your post."

"I know, but I wanted to watch the actors talk to the audience," I said.

"It's not your post," they said in unison. They were creepy, like Stepford Pages. I walked back to my chair, but before I left, I slipped my picture into the casting director's bag without her knowing.

After the taping ended, I was amazed by all the behind-the-scenes action. Tony Danza's agent had a really nice suit on, which made me want an agent with a nice suit. Tony himself came out on stage to say goodbye to the audience and answer questions—everybody just went crazy. They loved him. A woman shouted out, "Tony, can I see your ass?" He turned around and flexed his butt cheeks. He had a really well-toned butt for a forty-eight-year-old man.

I thought, *Geez, I should really do more squats.*

The next day, my boss called me up and fired me. "Why?" I asked.

"I just don't think the discipline is there," he said.

"What do you mean?" I said.

"I heard you left your station to watch the actors," he said.

"There was nothing for me to do," I said.

"You could have been cleaning up your post."

"But my post is a chair and a door."

"I'm sorry," he said. "I just don't think you have what it takes to be a page. Turn in your page jacket and page tie by Friday."

The Bastard Child of Robbie Benson and James Woods

I was getting nowhere. (Theme!) Then, Kelly said she knew a manager named Steven Scheinbaum who represented young people; he would take a look at my headshots. A guy from my acting class took some photographs of me at a downtown loft. I sent Steven a picture of me wearing a Richie Cunningham jacket and standing next to a graffiti-covered wall with a sneer on my face. I had this total pose going on, because I was trying to have edge and look tough. It was the stupidest picture ever taken.

Steven called me up and said, "After I saw your headshot, I had to call you in."

"Really?" I asked. "Why?"

"That sneer," he said. "It was different. There was something going on in that sneer." Who knew?

I had heard that you could never get anywhere with just a picture unless you were a supermodel, so this was a pleasant surprise. I went to Steven's office to meet with him. He looked at my résumé of lies and said, "*Man of La Mancha* . . . very impressive."

Steven told me that he liked to surf every weekend and work three days a week. "I don't need much," he said. "I've got two clients on *General Hospital* and I make my hundred and fifty Gs a year."

Steven was a cool guy, but the epitome of the Hollywood slacker representative. He was a fifty-one-year-old who didn't pick up the phone before ten, took a two-hour lunch, and left at six. One of those guys who loved the idea of being in show business, but didn't love to do the work. He talked big and thought small. He considered being a regular on *One Life to Live* to be the apex of an acting career.

But I didn't have anything going on, so I begged him to take me. He said I had an interesting quality, and he thought I could get some work. Then he introduced me to his partner, saying, "Hey Mel, look at this kid. If Robby Benson and James Woods had a baby, right?" They both laughed, but I didn't get the joke.

Steven represented me for about a year, but he didn't do much. I kept bugging him to send me out. Finally, he said, "Well, there's an open call for *In Living Color* this Saturday."

"What do I do?"

"Just show up."

I got to the Fox studio an hour early. The line was already ten blocks long. Every nut in the world was there. I waited in line for more than seven hours. Then, an assistant came outside and said, "We're only seeing twenty-five more people." There were over four hundred of us outside. Everyone started screaming and clamoring. It was a zoo. A comedian I knew named Brian Holtzman said, "Fuck you, Fox" and jumped on the back of a garbage truck that was pulling into the studio gates. I grabbed the other side of the truck. We kept our heads down and rode in, undetected. We ran into the *In Living Color* building and snuck into the line on the stairs. We were put in the final audition group. Finally, my turn came. I did two characters—Brad Gluckman, white Malibu rapper, and Fire Marshall Chuck, who was Fire Marshall Bill's younger brother. I got big laughs, so I thought I had a shot. Steven called them to follow up. A week later, they called back and said, "Who's Jamie Kennedy?"

That was one of maybe three auditions I had through Steven. I'd call him five times a day, and he wouldn't call me back for a week. When I finally got him on the phone, he'd tell me, "It's dead, kid. Kevin Costner's getting all the work." I'd be thinking, *Even the Sunny Delight commercials*?

I would go into his office and he'd tell me how he was surfing that morning, "Crazy waves out there, man. I caught my first half pipe at six A.M. It was so gnarly."

The whole time, I'd be thinking, *Why is he telling me this? Why isn't he getting me a* Beverly Hills 90210 *audition?* I mean, I was flat fucking broke. Then he would go off about how Jack

Nicholson was the best actor of all time. "Oh . . . *Chinatown* man? Forget it."

I'd think, *Jack Nicholson's good? Way to be dialed in, bro! I suppose next you'll tell me how Rock Hudson was gay.*

Steven was supportive, though. He believed in me—he just didn't believe in picking up the phone. At the end of the day, he surfed my career right down the toilet. Eventually, he stopped calling me and I stopped calling him. Actually, I just couldn't get ahold of him.

7.

Down and Out About a Mile or Two from Beverly Hills

He is happiest, be he king or peasant,
who finds peace in his home.
—Johann von Goethe

Living in a Hole in the Wall, Literally

My life was falling apart. My agent had fired me, I couldn't hold down a job, and my living situation was bleak. Koreatown was by far the worst neighborhood I had ever lived in. Every night I woke up to the sound of gunshots. The streets were always pitch black and the supermarkets sold only low-grade food. I couldn't walk anywhere without seeing crackhead hustlers and drunken bums splayed out on the curb.

The apartment itself was a dump. The whole place was maybe two hundred square feet, and I got twenty of it. My room was an old, boarded-up storage closet with a boxspring instead of a bed and the back of a leaking refrigerator coming through the wall. In order to get into the room, I had to crawl through a hole in the wall that Andy carved out. There was crap every-where—wood and bricks and dust. I was living like a goblin. For a few weeks, I couldn't even get my boxspring level because there was so much stuff on the floor. I just slept on an angle.

Andy knew girls would never have sex with him if they realized there was a goblin living inside his wall. So the rule was, if he brought back a girl, I wasn't allowed to make any noise or walk in and out of my room. Usually, I just snuck out of the apartment for a few hours before he got there. One time, he brought some girl home, then crept into my hole before I could get out of the place. "You can't leave," he said. "She's already naked and she'll freak out." So I was a prisoner of my hole. Actually, I was a prisoner of this girl's hole.

They immediately started to make sloppy, slurping sex noises. I had nothing in the room to distract myself—no books, no magazines. It was horrible. So I read the refrigerator manual, trying to drown out their moans of pleasure.

"Ooooh! Aaaah!" she screamed

"Oh, we have an automatic defrost," I read to myself. "How interesting."

"Oh god!" Andy moaned.

"And we have a crisper. Bet that comes in handy."

"JESUS! CHRIST! OHHHHHH!"

After two hours, she asked Andy, "Is there anything else I can do for you?" I was hoping he would say, "Yeah, there's a little goblin who lives in my wall. Can you get him an agent?" Instead, he asked for a ham sandwich. I picked up the warranty card of the refrigerator and continued reading.

I'm No Stool Pusher

Our landlord Karl was a closeted-homosexual Vietnam veteran who sounded *exactly* like Beetlejuice. His three favorite activities were talking about the war, hitting on me, and cooking disgusting meals. Every time I turned down his sexual advances or his food, he'd threaten to evict me. At least once a week, I'd open my door to find him standing there.

"Hey, I got some eggs. Do you want some?" he'd say.

I'd look down and see these runny yolks with old onions in them. "Nah, that's okay," I'd say.

"You don't like my cooking? Screw you, then. RENT'S DUE!" he'd say as he stormed off. An hour later, he'd be back. "Whatcha doing?" he'd ask.

"Nothing."

"You wanna talk?"

"About what?"

"I dunno."

"I can't right now," I'd say. Then I'd turn around and he'd grab my ass.

"Just wiping some lint off your pants," he'd say.

"I really wish you wouldn't do that."

"What, you want to be out living on the streets with all the weirdos and sickos? You're lucky you have a nice warm apartment here, with a hotplate," he'd say.

One night, he invited me over. I was starving and had absolutely no money. (Theme!) As a last resort, I decided to take him up on his offer. We were watching TV and eating eggs when he turned to me.

"They're good, right?" he asked.

"Yeah," I said.

"Do you want some beer?" he asked.

"No, I'm fine," I told him.

"Do you want some pot?"

"No, that's okay."

"Do you want a toot?"

"I'm good."

He was silent for a moment. Then he asked, "Can I squeeze your ass?"

I turned to him and said, "Karl, you say that like you're kidding. But you also seem like you're not kidding. And it makes me uncomfortable. Are you gay? If you are, that's cool. I'm okay with it."

"What?!" he said. "Do you think I'm some sort of faggot? Are you calling me a faggot?"

"Sorry," I said.

"I'm no stool pusher!" Then he turned to me, wistful. "I just get lonely sometimes, you know. Up here in this gated hellhole."

"Well, why don't you get a girl?" I asked.

"I dunno," he said. "Women talk too much. Besides, I just wanna catch a nut."

"Why don't you get a hooker?"

"WE'RE ALL FUCKING HOOKERS!" he shouted.

I went back to watching TV. Then, he turned to me. "So, can I squeeze your ass or not?"

There was only one way to distract him—bring up Vietnam. "So Karl, I bet you were a real sharp shooter in Da Nang."

He crossed his arms and said, "Pfffffffffft. I could hit a gook at two hundred yards."

That was a good beginning, but he still seemed interested in my ass. "Who do you think started that war, Karl?" I asked.

This was his hot button. He began to rant. "I'll tell you who started that goddamn war. Nelson Rockefeller. He started that goddamn war to sell helicopters. That's how he made all his money. The more war, the more people fighting, the more helicopters, the more money going in his pocket. He started the goddamn thing to pay his country club bills, that fucking asshole. Have another highball while I'm out here with Charlie in the goddamn rice paddies, you cocksucker!"

I just sat there, listening and eating my food. I thought his grabbing my ass and rambling on about Vietnam seemed like a small price to pay for free runny eggs.

Janeane's Little Maid Boy

I was flat broke. I took a job at a maid service called "You Got It Maid!" We maids could either work the morning or the afternoon shift. I always requested the morning shift in case I had an audition in the afternoon, which I never did. Basically, people would hire a maid to come into their house for four hours and clean it, which I always felt was really stupid, because if you're going to have a maid, it should be someone you know and trust.

It was yet another crappy job. I had a bitter, unsuccessful musician for a boss and my coworkers spoke no English. The company Christmas party was me and three little old ladies from Guatemala. I was a bad maid because I had nothing but contempt for anyone who was stupid enough to hire a starving actor to clean for them. I usually did a cursory cleaning, then made a sandwich and watched cable TV. Then I left two hours early.

One day, I got a call for a job at a house right off Melrose. The name on the work order was "Janeane Garofalo." I had actually met Janeane a year earlier, at Pizza Express in Beverly Hills, during the fifth or sixth comedy set I ever did. The club was run by this psycho woman MC who hated me and never gave me stage time. She claimed I wasn't a professional comic because I used to strip on stage. As far as I was concerned, it was a matter of artistic necessity. I mean, the place was ridiculous. Comedians had to yell jokes at the customers while they were eating veal scaloppini and meatballs. No one could ever get the audience to listen. So I would pull my pants down to get their attention.

Janeane showed up at Pizza Express to watch her friend, a girl who was just starting out on our circuit. I had heard Janeane's name before, because people were talking about how she was going to be the next big comedian. When she went on stage, she was really dry and funny. I thought she was cute, but I was too intimidated to approach her. I figured I would see her again, since we were both such up-and-comers on the circuit. A year later, I was cleaning her house.

I knocked on her door and Janeane answered in a towel. She smiled broadly and said, "Are you my little maid boy?"

"Yeah," I mumbled, grabbing my Tilex.

She pointed to a room and said, "Don't clean there. That asshole doesn't pay rent."

She was sharing. I saw my opening. "You know, I'm a comedian too," I blurted out.

She said, "Great! Make sure you clean the stove."

Then she left. The last thing I wanted to do was clean her place. All I wanted was to learn how she was succeeding in Hollywood. So I began snooping. I found an old laundry basket with tapes of her performances. Janeane on *Letterman*. Janeane on *Leno*. Janeane on *Larry Sanders*. I plopped down on the couch and watched them, studying how she did her setups. When I was done with that, I explored the rest of the house. Her bathroom was in bad shape. In normal apartments, we had to use a pre-scrub on the shower basin and then a scrub to get the mildew off the tiles. In Janeane's, I had to use three pre-scrubs just to get to the scrub.

I walked into her bedroom. In the center was a big fluffy bed covered with stuffed animals. There were a collection of Beanie Babies on display. I decided to go through her underwear drawer. Not because I was perverted. I just wanted to see how she was making it in show business. She had a lot of different styles, but for some reason fruit was a common panty motif. I didn't know what to make of it, so I continued snooping under the bed, in all her drawers, and in the closets, looking for some clue to her success. All I found were tampons.

Couldn't Afford Tears

My living situation grew tenser. Andy and I fought over the use of the hotplate, the shower privileges, and eventually, food. Once, he accused me of stealing the powdered cheddar from his individual macaroni and cheese packet. We had nothing in our refrigerator but condiments and ice cubes. My life had become truly pathetic.

Then, an oasis in the desert. I had been doing standup almost every night for a year. At the time, there was a new Monday night show at the Improvisation in Santa Monica, called New Faces Night. The Improv was one of the last great bastions of stand up comedy. To be there was to be with the best, so I decided to try out. I went to the Improv on a Monday at five P.M. There were already fifty comics there, waiting. We all put our name in a hat. The owner drew names out, one by one, and gave us the next available date for our auditions. We would each get five minutes to audition for the owner onstage, in front of a real paying crowd. If we did well at our auditions, the owner would put us on the Improv's regular rotation and give us a guaranteed spot or two each week.

I had three weeks until my showcase, so I went all over town, practicing my five-minute act. I thought it was really tight. After I auditioned, the owner told me that I didn't have a hook—something that would draw people in. He said I couldn't reaudition until I came up with one. I was pretty bummed, but there was an upside: a comic who was highly revered on the standup circuit saw my audition. He sent one of his people over to tell me, "Jamie, congratulations. Johnny Taco has decided to work with you."

"Really?" I said. "Why?"

"He sees potential in your act," the minion said. The deal was that I would give Johnny rides to gigs and he would be my mentor. He was from New York, hated cars, and didn't have a driver's license. I agreed.

Johnny and I had a strategy session. He broke it down for me: "You've got good hair, good teeth, bad skin, and no act. You're young, you're fun, you wear your hat backwards, you're dumb. That's your hook. You're young dumb Jamie Kennedy. All your jokes will be about being young, and how dumb you are." Let me tell you . . . this was a dumb idea. But I went with it. We worked on an act, got about six minutes of really dumb "dumb jokes," and made everything tight.

The audience LOVED it, although I think they were just laughing because they thought I had cerebral palsy. I mean, one of my best jokes was, "What did the elephant say to the kangaroo? I don't know, 'cause I'm an idiot." Then I went into a corner and put a dunce hat on. The owner came up to me after my next audition and said, "Congratulations, you've got yourself a hook. I'll give you some spots." I was thrilled. I got to go up every Monday night and do my dumb act. The crowds were good and it was really exciting.

Then, I woke up one day to find my car missing. At first I thought it was stolen. Then I learned that the City of Los Angeles had towed it, due to nonpayment of eight hundred dollars worth of parking tickets. (I hadn't paid a single parking ticket since I'd gotten to LA—I would just throw them out the window and think nothing of it.) Getting the car back would have cost more than I paid for it originally. Besides, I didn't have that kind of cash. Once again, I was stranded.

Things quickly went downhill from there. I couldn't make it to the Improv on the bus, so I couldn't commit to my spots. Then, Johnny Taco decided that he didn't want to work with me any more.

"Why?" I asked him.

"You don't need me. You're fine," he said. "You've got a great dumb hook."

Then, he found another young comic to mentor. A guy who drove a Nissan. Suddenly, it hit me: Johnny Taco had just been using me for my ride.

————

I finagled another car, an old Ford Fairmont. The owner let me pay her off, little by little. Since I'd been out of the Improv loop for about three months, I had lost my place in the pecking order, and would have to reaudition in a month. In the meantime, I needed to make some money because Andy moved out, leaving me with the entire $180 per month rent payment. I got myself a job performing as a clown at kids' birthday parties, making balloon animals and doing other clown-related activities. I kept all my clown gear in the backseat: my wig, my big nose, and my big shoes. One day, I came out of my apartment and saw that someone had broken into my car the night before. They had smashed the window, opened up the dashboard, and taken my license. Not only that, but they had also stolen all my clown gear—and smeared shit all over my car. Human feces. I have no idea why. I envisioned a crackhead with a diarrhea problem walking around town, making balloon animals, going, "Hey, wanna giraffe, muthafucka?"

The next day, a lady in a BMW rear-ended me. I had no insurance, and the woman tried to blame it on me.

The day after that, the transmission died.

All of this happened within three days. I thought, *Nothing else could possibly go wrong*.

The next day I was awoken at seven in the morning by the earsplitting sound of gears and hydraulics. I looked outside and realized that my car was being towed—I had accidentally parked it on the wrong side of the street. I ran out into the pouring rain, wearing only my underwear. "Please," I begged the driver. "Don't take my shit-smeared car! Please!" He wouldn't listen. I could do nothing but watch helplessly as he towed it off.

I walked back into my apartment, thinking about how I had nothing. No car, no agent, no career, no girlfriend, no money, no clown shoes. I opened the refrigerator. There was nothing in there but ketchup. I had *nothing*.

I went into my room. When I first moved in, I had written out my goals for the year and hung them on my walls for inspiration, alongside pictures of famous actors who I wanted to emulate. These things were supposed to remind me that this was all just part of the struggle. If living in a hole in the wall and sleeping on a boxspring was what you had to do to make it, so be it. Now, my optimism seemed stupid. Why didn't I just quit already? What was the point? I'd been in LA for almost two and a half years and I hadn't gotten anywhere. I didn't know if I'd ever make it.

I locked myself in the bathroom and sat on the toilet. I wanted to cry, but I couldn't. I didn't even have tears.

Owwwww

My roommate Andy was a very industrious guy. He always told me, "If you want to be an actor, you've gotta be proACTive." Andy himself looked exactly like Woody Harrelson, so he used to hang around the *Cheers* set, claiming that he was Woody's long-lost brother and could play that part on a show. I watched him and thought, *He really knows how to hustle.* Andy even signed with an agent. The guy handled actors who didn't speak but were featured—one step above being an extra. The agency just signed actors based on their physical look.

Then, Andy got sick of Hollywood and moved to Louisiana to be a blackjack dealer on a riverboat. A month after he left, the agency called to offer Andy a job. I had no way of getting in touch with him. So, using what he'd taught me, I lied and said that I *was* Andy. They gave me the gig. A 1-800-TheLaw2 commercial. Just like that, I became a working actor.

It was my very first on-camera acting job in LA. In the commercial, I played the guy in the front seat of a car who gets rear-ended. All I remember is snapping my neck back and going, "Owwwww!" Then, the other actor walked up to the car, pointed his finger at my face and said, "You've been hurt!"

They paid me two hundred and twenty bucks in cash, which was like manna from heaven. I used it to get my Ford Fairmont back from the towyard. This would be my last paid acting job for the next two and a half years.

Aug 13, 1992

I'm so depressed today. I'm sitting here on a bus. I feel like a helpless loser. I feel that as an actor, I'm not interesting and I'm not funny. I feel if my parents were to die tomorrow, that I would become a hopeless derelict, lost in the loop, and I would get fat and ugly. I feel like I can't stand on my own two feet. I want to stand on my own two feet more than anything.

8.

Sex, Drugs, and Acting Class

The first prerogative of an artist in any medium
is to make a fool of himself.
—Pauline Kael

Right Now You're Just a Shitty Waiter

At this point, I was taking an adult acting class. The school was at a busy intersection in Hollywood, and everyone used to practice their monologues outside, shouting at the top of their lungs as cars drove by. I would walk up to the building for my class, and there'd be some dude in leather outside, screaming a monologue from *All My Children* at a telephone pole.

I wasn't happy with the class, but I didn't do anything about it until I started dating Celerie. She was a standup comedienne who I had met a few months before at an open mic night at Gorky's Deli. Here's a free piece of advice: never touch a girl who touches a microphone. They're all Fruit Loops.

At first, I had no idea that Celerie was loony. I just thought she was really attractive, bright and funny. She was like the Jewish Julia Roberts, which I guess made her Barbra Streisand. Then we had sex for the first time. After it was over, Celerie started to cry.

"What's wrong?" I asked.

"It just brings back memories," she said.

"Of who?" I asked.

"My dad."

I just hugged her and thought, *Oh my God, I want out of here*. Celerie had mommy issues, daddy issues, and basic world issues, but I ended up dating her anyway, because she was a good joke writer.

Celerie knew that I wasn't getting anything out of my acting class. She told me that if I wanted to learn how to act, I needed to go to a real acting school. My class was just a scene study workshop. It wasn't so much about learning the craft of acting as it was about getting jobs. That was the good thing about Celerie—she was really smart. And funny. She just needed a little lithium.

Celerie suggested that I check out a place called the Joan Baron/D.W. Brown studio. The studio taught the Meisner method of acting, which was developed by Sanford Meisner, one of the pioneers of the American acting style. At first, I thought the place seemed iffy. I had never heard of them, they didn't advertise, and the only way to get in was by referral. Also, they wouldn't let you audit a class. Instead, you had to sign up for a six week course and pay $600. After that, you could enter the school's two-year program, if you so chose. When I went to an informational meeting, the place was packed. Still, I didn't know about the $600 fee, so Celerie said, "Audit another class and then decide."

So I audited a class at another school, and it scared me. The teacher was harsh. He seemed to get off on bullying his students. An actor was onstage doing an emotional, difficult exercise and the teacher said, "Bill, what do you want to be?"

Bill said, "An actor."

The teacher said, "Well, right now you're just a shitty waiter."

He also brought his personal life into the class. Like, a girl and a guy were doing a scene that depicted a fight between a married couple. The teacher stopped the girl, screaming, "Cut, cut, cut! You're supposed to be a dumb whore in this scene. Well, act like a dumb whore. Let me help you."

He ripped her top and turned to the guy, "I hate stupid actors. I hate them, I hate them! Keep poking her, keep poking her, goddamnit. You know what? Let me do it. I'll show you how to act this goddamn scene. So let's pretend you're my wife, who, incidentally, just left me, and I still owe you child support payments. Even though I just caught you sucking Warren's cock in my bed. MY FUCKING BED!"

"Is that in the script?" the actress asked.

"It's in *my* fucking script, okay? And it wasn't just one blowjob. He fucked her! Ready? Say action, somebody. I'm gonna show you how to treat a dumb whore!"

"Action!" I yelled out.

The teacher spewed out a parade of profanities. "Slut, whore, bitch, cunt, hate, piss, malice, I fucking hate you, you're the scum at the bottom of the condom!"

He turned to the actress, "Now, how do you feel?"

Her lower lip trembled and she started to bawl.

He said, "Oh you're gonna cry now, you big baby? You pathetic little field mouse?"

Back to the class, gentle and sincere, he said, "See there, class? That's the work. Isn't it beautiful? Tears streaming down her face, totally connected to her pain. Great job, Wendy. Just an announcement, guys: fees are due May first."

I decided to give Baron/Brown a shot. I was able to convince my parents to give me the money because it was a prestigious school with a challenging curriculum. As soon as I had my first turn in front of the class, I felt at home.

Their method was all about exposing the subtext of a scene, using acting to say the unsaid. The class was about learning how to get in touch with who you were, so that you could get in touch with who the character was. They taught us that acting was about replicating honest human emotional reactions. This was something that all of us had the potential to do, but society taught us very early on to hide our feelings. Here, we unlearned and discovered how to accept and show our true feelings instead. No covering up—just being raw.

For the first five months, we didn't even do scenes. We just did acting exercises that taught us how to read people's behavior by being attentive and listening. This required a lot of collaborative work. At my first class, our teacher announced, "You will be paired up with a partner with whom you will have to rehearse for a minimum of three times a week."

I raised my hand and asked, "What if you're a better actor than your partner?"

He stopped and said, "Boy, you have a lot to learn." I really thought it was a valid question. He continued, "There is no good and bad here. There's only truth. Anyone can be a good actor, as long as their acting comes from a truthful place within themselves."

After taking this class, I really came to believe it. Anybody can be a good actor if they show who they really are. An honest person is engaging to watch.

Cry Birdie Cry

Acting class really encouraged me to approach my life differently. It taught me to live in the moment, experiment, and see where things took me—to be open, without expectations. This led to some interesting experiences, to say the least. I was with my scene partner, Mitch, rehearsing a scene for class from a play called *The Dumbwaiter*. I opened his refrigerator and saw all these weird-looking mushrooms with long stems. "Dude, what are these?" I asked.

"Shrooms."

"Oh, I've heard about them. What do they do?"

"They enlighten you. Do you want to take them?"

"I don't know, dude."

"It'll help you with your acting."

"Okay, let's take them."

"I've had them for over a year," he said. "I don't know if they're still any good."

We went to Koo Koo Roo, a restaurant, and ordered a bunch of chicken. Then we mixed the mushrooms into some salads—about three stems each. We played hoops, rehearsed some more, and drove around. About three hours later I said, "Dude, I don't feel anything."

"Yeah, I think they're old," Mitch said. "Let's go to the movies."

We went to see Francis Ford Coppola's *Dracula*. The theater was packed, and there weren't any seats together, so we split up. As soon as I sat down, I felt different. Kinda tingly. I thought, "Man, this film is gonna be AMAAAAZZZING."

Was it ever. Pure genius. I cried the whole time. Gary Oldman played a dog bat. He kept crying because Winona Ryder kept rebuffing his love. I kept standing up, screaming and crying at the screen like a big black woman, "I feel your pain, dog bat!" I was tripping my brains out.

Mitch walked over to me at the end of the movie. He was crying too. We stared at each other, tears streaming down our cheeks. I couldn't speak. He nodded his head, put his hand on my shoulder like a priest, and said, "I know. I know."

I remember when I was young and I would cry everyday and I would say the day was good if I didn't cry. Girl just called me weird.

Learn to be present now is what they teach you! During that movie I kept monitoring myself and saying Don't END, this is great; instead of enjoying Now! Every woman was a beauty even when she came down the stairs all bloody without her head.

Shrooms are one of the best things creation has given us. They are incredible. I saw everything for its true beauty. Look past the flesh and into their souls! I was all MAN!

She spit blood in his face. She was still pretty. I want to be a vampire, lay around all day, eat grapes and have sex with other vampires!

Dracula was love, passion, beauty. No judgement. It was what it was. It was women at their height and men at theirs. It was all one. It was Winona beautiful. She will suck you in and you will be with her always. Gary Oldman was passion. He made Winona the center of his world. She was all encompassing.

The beauty of her skin was indescribable. Even
a zit on her ~~surface~~ face would be beautiful. She
was Oxyfree. Keanu was handsome. A strong
chin kept him along he was. It was a
ride that will never end, don't end, go on go
just fly birdie fly. Run with your emotion.
Cry birdie, Cry! Don't use math! Go with
your guts. Internal organs. Your spine is
intertwined. Follow spirts beyond! GO!!
     I'd like to find a peice of mind.
Dracula and Shrooms have changed my
life!

Food Whore

I was very taken with my acting class. It was the best experience I'd had since moving to LA. I wanted to get as much out
of the process as I could, so I decided to really focus and put all
my efforts into becoming a better actor. To that end, I decided
to become celibate; I was basically celibate anyway, but this
time it was by choice. The combination of being extremely
receptive to new experiences and not having sex for a year was
an interesting one. While this did help harness my energy, it
also got me into some very odd situations.

Maggie was a girl in my acting class who always used to
stare at me. A nice girl, but I never thought anything of it—she
was Australian, married, and way too skinny. Maggie was also
a vegan, but she pronounced it with a soft g, like vejan. She
lived off of nuts and lemon rinds. One day in class, the two of
us were partnered up to do yoga stretching exercises. I had
been taking the class for a while and knew all the different
poses, so I was able to stretch her out pretty well. I must
have stretched out her g-spot or something (or as she would

call it, her j-spot) because what happened next came out of nowhere.

After class, she came up to me. "I just want to thank you for stretching me," she said.

"Sure, no problem," I said.

"You know, we should switch numbers and hang out sometime."

"For, like, acting?" I asked. I was completely oblivious (and celibate).

"Exactly," she said.

I gave her my number—and then she kissed me goodbye. But it was a weird kiss. It was one of those kisses when the other person goes cheek and you start to go cheek and then at the last minute the other person goes lips and you're like, *Whoa, why are we at lips? I thought we were at cheek.* And then you're all tangled up. In fact, the kiss was doubly weird, because she kind of lingered there and sucked on my bottom lip. I was shocked to be getting bottom lip suction. But I still had no idea what she meant by it. God, was I stupid.

The next day, Maggie phoned and asked me to meet her at a coffee shop. We talked about acting class, but she kept staring through me while she was eating her soy nuts, like she was one of the Children of the Corn. Finally she said, "Maybe we should hang out."

"Well, aren't we already hanging out?" I asked.

"Yeah, but a little bit more," she said.

"You mean like . . . more time?"

"Sort of," she said.

"Maybe," I said. I was slowly starting to realize that she wanted more than a double foam latte. A week later, she called me again. It was after midnight.

"I'm coming to see you," she said.

"Why?" I said.

"To hang out," she said.

"I can't. I'm rehearsing," I said.

"Hey Jamie," she said. "You're broke, right? You probably haven't eaten a decent meal in a while. Why don't I take you out for dinner?"

"Reaaallly?" I said.

"Mmmm-hmmmm."

"Welllllll, can we go anywhere?"

"Mmmm-hmmmm."

"Italian?"

"Mmmm-hmmmm."

"I'll meet you downstairs in ten minutes."

Maggie picked me up and took me to an Italian restaurant in the Valley. I loaded my plate with chicken parmigiana, linguine, and bread. I started stuffing food down my face. I finished it off with a nice piece of tiramisu. She kept trying to move closer to me as I attempted to eat. I'd take a bite, she'd shift her chair a few inches toward me, I'd back away. This went on until I was full. Then, she drove me home. She pulled over outside my apartment building.

"Okay, thanks!" I said. "See you later!"

"Wait! I just want to talk to you!"

"What do you want to talk about?" I asked.

She shrugged. We sat in uncomfortable silence for a moment. Finally I said, "Did you hear about Prince Charles? He tore his ACL in a polo match!"

"I'm not British, you drongo, I'm Australian," she said.

"Oh really? Well, what about Margaret Thatcher's new—"

Then she tried to kiss me.

"No!" I pulled away. "You're married. I have strict morals."

"Don't throw a wobbly. I just want to kiss you."

"Well, we can't. No way."

"Well, you have to do something," she said. "I just bought you that whole bloody fucking meal. You owe me."

"What am I? A food whore?"

"No, but you owe me."

"What do you want to do?" I asked. I knew what she wanted, but I was stalling for time.

"Let me touch your chest."

I figured that she was right—I had to put out. Chest-touching seemed a fair barter. "Fine," I said.

Maggie unbuttoned my shirt and started rubbing. "Ooooooh," she moaned. "This feels nice." Then she put her head over my heart. "Oh god, I can feel your heart beating," she said.

"That's where . . . the heart is," I said.

"It's so amazing."

"Cool. Well, I'm going upstairs now," I said. "Good night."

"Aren't you going to invite me up?"

"I told you I can't. You're married."

"But it's no big deal," she said. "In Australia everyone bed hops."

"Well, not in America," I said indignantly.

Maggie pulled back and stared at the single hair on my chest. "Ooooh, that hair," she said. Then she plucked it. I screamed in pain. "Now it's completely clean!" she said. "Like a freshly mowed field."

That was it. I ran upstairs, vowing to never let anything like that happen again. I was raised a strict Catholic and had visions of myself burning in hell with the devil pouring lighter fluid all over me.

I continued to go to class. And I continued to be really broke. Then, Maggie got me a few jobs as an assistant at her husband's law firm. The husband was a high-powered lawyer who traveled a lot, so she was often lonely. He turned out to be a nice little guy who looked like a mixture of Sid Vicious and Howdy Doody, with a really high voice and a falsetto accent. I really liked him, and my commitment to not sleeping with Maggie doubled.

One day after class, Maggie asked me to go get veggie burgers and smoothies. I felt weird, but I was hungry, so I went. On the drive home, Maggie pulled over in front of some building. She really wanted to mess around. When I said no, she started to get a little nuts.

"What's your problem?" she yelped. "I fucking help you so much. I'm the only one who helps you." It was true. "I want to mess around right now. Or I'm not giving you a ride home."

I said, "All right. Just a kiss. Let's get it over with."

She took me into the back of her Range Rover. We pushed down the seats and covered the windows with our jackets, so nobody could see us. I was so paranoid and egocentric, like somebody was going to walk down the street and say, "Hey, look at the homeless actor and the Aussie vegan making out!"

The whole time Maggie and I were kissing, I kept thinking about how we were committing a cardinal sin. I was going to burn in hell for this. I mean, yes, it was possible that I was already going to hell for having had premarital sex in the past, but adultery was so much worse. And what would my mom say if I ended up in hell? She'd be beyond disappointed. Plus, I had just seen this movie starring Juliette Binoche and Jeremy Irons called *Damage*. In the movie, Jeremy Irons sleeps with his son's girlfriend and then the son jumps off a balcony. And I started thinking, *If her husband finds out, he's going to jump off a balcony.* Then I thought about how, in the movie, Jeremy Irons continues to sleep with his son's fiancée even though his son is a quadriplegic, which I thought was an extremely shitty move.

Needless to say, with all this running through my mind, I wasn't exactly enjoying myself. I felt so guilty that I kept ducking every time a car drove by. "What are you so worried about?" she finally said.

"Your husband."

"He doesn't even know I'm alive," she said.

I had to stop.

Maggie dropped me off. I said, "That's it. It's over."

Afterwards I was really upset by the whole experience. The only way I could make myself feel better was to justify it through religion. I said to myself, *Okay, the Lord says do unto others as you'd have done to you. So if I get married and the worst thing that my wife ever does is make out with some guy in the back of a Range Rover . . . well, I can live with that.* I resolved never to get myself in this position again.

A few days after Maggie and I had our makeout session, my car broke down on the side of the road. I didn't have anyone I could call, except her. Maggie picked me up and drove me to my apartment. Then she turned off the car. *Oh shit,* I thought.

"What are you doing?" I asked.

"Well, I picked you up," she said. "Time to pay."

"Aw, c'mon," I said.

"Can't I come up?" she said. "I won't do anything. I swear."

I brought Maggie to my apartment, where she attempted to grope me. I couldn't take it. "Please, stop!" I said. "I can't. It's a sin."

"It's not a sin," she said. "It's pleasure. It's fun. Sin again!"

"I can't!" But then a year's worth of hormones took over. I started to think, *If the worst thing that ever happened in my marriage was that a guy made out with my wife and fondled her tits a little . . . I guess it would be okay. I can live with that.*

I kissed her. Then, she stuck her hand down my pants. I screamed, "NO! I can't! It's a sin!"

"It's not a sin!" she said. "Doesn't it feel good?"

"Well . . . kinda."

Then I thought, *Okay, if the worst thing my wife does is play with another man's penis, I can live with that.* We kept making out. She took off my pants and then hers. Her vagina was completely bald. It freaked me out. I had never seen anything like it.

"Oh my god!" I said. "What happened to you?"

"I shaved it," she said. "It's cleaner that way. Now touch me. Please touch me."

"I can't," I said. "It looks like a baby pussy. That makes it even more of a sin!"

She grabbed my hand, put it inside of her and started moaning. I thought, *Okay, if the worst thing that happens is that my wife has some guy put his fingers in her, I can live with that. As long as his hands are clean.* We kept messing around.

Then Maggie said, "Let's have sex."

"No way," I said. "I can't live with my wife doing that."

"What wife? You're not married."

"I know," I said. "But in the future."

"Oh fuck," she said, exasperated. "Just stick it in."

"I can't!"

This went on for the next five minutes. She kept asking and I kept saying no. Finally, she sat up and glared at me. "You know what, Jamie?" she said, "It's all technicalities at this point. You've already committed the fucking sin. You're going to BURN."

Bam! It hit me like a ton of bricks. She was right—I'd already done something awful. I was an adulterer. I made her get dressed and walked her to her car. "I can't do this again," I said.

"No, I must see you!" she said. "My husband is so bloody boring. I hate him." I put her in her car and told her to go.

It was two A.M. I stayed up all night, a total wreck. I kept thinking, *I've sinned. I'm going to hell. This is it.*

Maggie called me at six A.M. "I must see you!" she said.

"Maggie, no."

"My husband's here," she said. "I hate him! I hate him so much!"

"Hon," her husband said in the background, totally benign. "It's a beautiful morning. Should we go for a jog?"

"FUCK YOU!" she screamed at him. "YOU'RE A FUCK-ING BASTARD!" Then she said to me in a shaky voice, "Do you see what I mean? He's a fucking sheila. I fucking hate him. I love you, though. God, I love you."

Meanwhile, I had known her for twelve days. Her husband was like the perfect gentleman. "I can't see you anymore," I said.

"Well," she said, "Then all I can tell you is . . . I don't know what's going to happen."

"What do you mean?" I said.

She started to cry. "I don't know what I'll do with myself," she said. "I'm unstable right now."

"Maggie," I said. "Don't say that."

"Then let me come over," she sobbed.

I sighed. "Fine."

"Okay, be over in ten!" she said, suddenly perky.

Maggie showed up at my apartment, all crying and skinny and vegan. "I'm going to kill myself," she wailed. "I'm really gonna do it. It's all your fault."

"Maggie," I said. "You don't even know me."

"That's it. I'm jumping out the window!" she said.

"It's only five feet down. All you'll do is break your ankle."

"I don't care," she said, running over to the window. Sobbing, she tried to remove the screen. I pulled it out of her hands. She punched me in the chest, kicked me in the balls, and ran out of my apartment.

I locked my door, took a shower, and went to sleep. Three hours later, I got up to go to the gym. I walked out of my building and found Maggie crying on my steps.

"You've been here the whole time?" I asked.

"Yes," she sniffed. "My heart's been through a fucking meat grinder."

"I've known you for two weeks," I said. "All I've done is eat carbohydrates in your presence. Your husband loves you. Go home to him."

She got up and walked away.

I saw her husband once after that, a few years later. He was still really nice to me. He said, "I've just seen you in a commercial, mate. You're doing quite well. Congratulations." I don't think he ever knew. I felt like the world's biggest crumb.

Scared Shitless

Once I entered my self-discovery stage, I became very open to all that the world had to offer me—and not just in terms of acting. One day, I saw an ad in a newspaper for free colon hydrotherapy. The deal was that this guy would give you a free colonic and then you would have a therapy session. His theory was that if you had a clear colon, you'd have a clear conscience, which would allow you to go deeper in psychoanalysis. Sounded good on paper. I was broke and someone was offering me colonic enlightenment—for free!

I called him right away. It was about nine-thirty on a Tuesday night. He came to the phone immediately. "Hey, how you doin'?" he asked.

"Hey," I said. "I want to come in for an appointment."

"When?"

"The sooner the better," I told him. I was raring to go.

"You're lucky," he said. "My client just cancelled. You can come over right now."

"Tonight? Cool!" I said.

He gave me an address on North Gardener Street. "Is there a hospital on that street?" I asked.

"No, today I'm just doing it out of my office."

"Okay." I hopped into my car and drove over, not thinking that there was anything weird about the fact that he was
willing to meet with me at ten-thirty on a Tuesday night. When
I drove up, I realized that I was in a very residential area. His
house had all these antennas in the backyard. Not just TV
antennas. These were forty foot NASA-type satellite antennas.
Like he was trying to communicate with Neptune or Planet
Xenon or something. I thought, *Okay, that's a little weird. But hey,
I'm going to get a free colonic!*

I parked the car and got out. His house was the only one
on the block that had gates on every window. They were made
of reinforced steel. It was like a fortress. I thought, *This is definitely weird, but I'm getting a free colonic!*

I walked up to the door, which bore a large handgun
sticker. It read, "The Exterminator." I started to get a little
freaked out, but I rang the doorbell anyway. The colon guy
answered. He was like six foot five, three hundred pounds,
with a huge beer gut. And he was wearing overalls. His bottom
teeth looked like they were fused to together, like one big
chunk of tartar.

"You're right on time," he said. "Come into my office."

I walked in. The place was pitch black. It was a total
dump—Chinese takeout cartons, boxes of books, animal heads
on plaques, shotgun shells. And guns everywhere. I thought,
Oh fuck. This is the fat Jeffrey Dahmer!

He said, "Pardon the mess. I'm doing some reconstruc-
tion." I didn't see a single tool. Just dirt and garbage. "Have a
seat," he said. "And please fill out this form. I'll need some
basic information."

He handed me a questionaire hand-written on the back of
an Old Navy receipt. I hesitated and asked him, "I'm sorry . . .
can I see some credentials?"

"Okay," he said, a little perturbed. "Follow me."

I followed him back to his office, down this dark hallway. I thought, *This is like* Silence of the Lambs. *And I'm gonna be that girl in the hole.* We walked into his office. There were like ten diplomas from Devry. He shone a flashlight on them, revealing hundreds of boxes of bullets on the floor. I was going to be shot, filleted, and eaten.

"You know what? I don't think I'm gonna do this," I said.

"Up to you, but a clean colon is a happy colon," he said.

I started inching toward the door. "I'm cool," I said.

A moment of uncomfortable silence. Then he whispered, "You know what? You're getting a colonic whether you like it or not."

I screamed like a five-year-old girl and bolted out the door, down the street and into my car.

Later I told my friends what I'd done. They said I was the dumbest person on the planet. But what was I supposed to do? It was a free colonic! Who would have known? And maybe that was all part of his method. Because he literally did scare the shit out of me.

Brave Little Herpes Flower

My standup act improved, so other comics began including me in their shows. One night, I was performing late at the Comedy Store with my friend Charlie, who was also a waiter at Nate-n-Al's. Sharon, one of Charlie's fellow employees from the restaurant, came to see him. I was immediately attracted to her, so after my set, I invited her out for tea. At this point, my hair was really long and grungy—I was getting in touch with my "inner artist." Plus, I wanted to look like Kurt Cobain. Sharon said to Charlie, "He's cute, but why doesn't he ever take a shower? Is he clean?"

"Yeah, he's pretty clean," Charlie said.

She decided to go. By this time, I had taken acting class long enough to perfect my skills as a bullshit artist. I looked into her eyes, all actory-deep, and said, "I know what kind of tea you want."

"Yeah?"

"You don't want tea. You just want to be loved."

Then her eyes welled up and she nodded her head "yes." It was so stupid. Sharon really fell for it. She thought I could see into her soul. Truth is, all I could see into was her blouse. Luckily, she saw me have a good set that night. If she saw me bomb, I never would have gotten to have sex with her, no matter how deeply I looked into her eyes.

Later that night, we were driving around in my car, listening to the radio and snuggling. Then, a public service announcement came on. "And remember, most people don't know they have herpes," the announcer said. "Get tested!"

"Boy, I'm glad that's not us," I said, joking around.

Out of nowhere, she started to cry.

"What's wrong?" I asked.

"I have herpes," she said.

"No way!" I said.

"Every time I have sex with someone I have to tell them that I have herpes," she wailed. "I haaaaaaaate it."

"No way!" I said.

"Yeah, I got it from this jerk," she said. "I slept with him and he didn't tell me he had it. I hate him."

"No way!"

"Yeah."

At first I was turned off. Then, scared. Then, I felt bad for her. I realized that she had to drag herself through the mud every time she wanted to have sex. I thought, *This girl is really brave. We all have our crosses to bear, but she has to bear hers on her vagina.* But I still was too scared to sleep with her. She got mad at me, so I went to a clinic to see if I could learn how to work around the herpes. There, the strangest coincidence happened.

When I was looking for information, I met some guy who was researching the exact same thing. He'd had the same exact experience as me—and on the exact same night. I thought it was amazing.

I said, "Do you think that God put us both here so we would each have someone to talk to about this?"

"Uh, no," he said. "I think it's because we're both at a herpes clinic."

"Oh." I grabbed my pamphlet with the herpes hotline number and split.

It took a while before I got up the courage to sleep with Sharon—I really had to educate myself before I could go there. After a few weeks, I was ready. Sharon and I went into the bedroom and started messing around. "Put it in," she whispered. "I'm fine."

"One second," I whispered back. Then, I picked up the phone and called the herpes hotline. "Okay, I'm ready to penetrate my partner," I said.

"Sir, do you have a condom on your penis?" the herpes hotline woman asked.

"I do."

"Do you have spermicidal gel on your thighs?"

"Yes."

"Is your partner clear of outbreak?"

"Yes."

"You're clear for entry, sir."

Finally, we had sex. Sharon turned out to be an animal in bed, complete with biting and clawing. When she came, she screamed at me like Rob Zombie and said, "Let me see your face, you motherfucker! Look at me! LOOK AT ME!"

After a few months, Sharon broke up with me. She caught me stealing food out of her refrigerator. I guess she wasn't infected with generosity.

A poem I wrote for Sharon:

THE HERPES POEM   March 18, 1993

You brave little flower
With your secret to share
Knowing quite well
I may not care.
Yet you push forward
And spill your guts
You walk through the mire
Every time you meet
Some one New
"OH GOD, not Again"
You scream
"I have HERPES!!!"
Curse the skank of man
Who cast this on you.
For you were a little flower
Growing nice and straight
And he was the bee
Who stole your pollen
Yet you still forgive him
Although he'll never admit it
Your heart is as big
As the Grand Canyon
And that's why you're
The brave little herpes flower

Orgy At Eight, No Dairy

I had no more women to mooch food off of, but I still had to eat.
I "lucked" into a waitering position at a vegetarian restaurant in

Beverly Hills called The Tofu Hut. I went into the restaurant to audition for their Friday night comedy show. The owner, a fat Italian guy from New York said, "You're not funny. But I could use a waiter." This guy was like the Tony Soprano of vegetarianism. He swore if anyone stole his recipes he would have them killed. Whenever a beautiful woman would come into the restaurant, he'd whisper, "Oooh, I'd like to show her my soy dog."

It was the most demeaning job I'd ever had. He kept asking me, "So, you're a comic, huh?" and then telling me vegetarian jokes, like, "What's the difference between boogers and broccoli? Kids don't eat broccoli!" All his jokes were vegan. His setups were about tempeh and his punch line was always a vegetable. After he finished his joke, he'd threaten me, "Don't even *think* of stealing my material."

Ron Jeremy, this short, fat, hairy, extremely famous porn star, used to come in all the time. The owner treated him like royalty. He'd turn to the restaurant and announce, "Hey everyone, it's Ron Jeremy!" Like we were in Romper Room. Then the owner would whisper in my ear, "Listen, don't screw this up. Give Ron anything he wants."

I'd go up to Ron Jeremy's table and ask, "Can I help you?"

"Yeah," he'd say. "I want apple juice. But it has to be organic. No chemicals. Okay?"

"Absolutely," I'd say.

"Okay," he'd continue. "And I want the falafel. Steamed, not fried. Steamed."

"Sure," I'd say.

"And I want the organic baby leaf lettuce with the organic tofu and cheese. But not dairy cheese. Soy cheese. I can't have dairy. It clogs your intestines."

In the middle of ordering, he'd get a phone call on his cell phone: "Okay, you need me at three o'clock? Anal sex scene? No condom? How many girls? Four? Sure, I can do that."

He'd put the phone down for a moment, then say to me, "The pumpkin pie. Yeah. Is the crust organic rice crust or wheat crust? Because I don't do wheat."

Back on the phone, "Another scene at four-thirty? Two guys and a girl? Okay, that's good for me. But I'm not going to touch him or blow him, right? I don't do gay. Okay, I'll see you in a bit. Yes, I'll wash my balls before I go. Bye."

Then, back to me, "Do you have any Spirulina?"

Seven years later, I ran into Ron Jeremy at the *Scream 3* premiere. He was with two girls who looked like they really hated their life in porn. I tried to get him into the after-party, but I couldn't. He said, "Thanks anyway," and told me he was a big fan of my work. It was surreal.

Jamie's Celebrity Dream Journal

In acting class, we were encouraged to document our dreams. They were supposed to be the doorway to our hidden thoughts and motivations. My dreams were all about celebrities. Apparently, I had no subconscious.

Jan, 3, 1992

I had a dream last nite that I was with Oliver Stone and we were getting actors together for a Shakespeare movie that he was going to produce. Ben Kingsley, Ralph Fiennes, Liam Neeson, Daniel Day Lewis, Ian McKellen, and me. I told him his movie was great, but it didn't do well in test screenings.

March 11, 1992

I just had a dream that woke me up. The devil was standing over me breathing. His hot breath almost blew me out of bed, but I had the power of the Holy Spirit to keep me strong. I looked up, the devil was now Antonio Banderas. It was very real. I woke up hot and trembling.

June 10, 1992

I had a dream that I saw Jay Leno at a New Year's Eve party. He was bartending. ~~He was~~ I was talking to him about getting on the show. I told him I auditioned and he wasn't thrilled. Then he changed into Roseanne Barr. A group of fraternity guys were out there getting wasted and one was throwing up in a →

water fountain. I thanked Roseanne, but then she turned into Rosie O'Donnell. Then Rosie said she going to give something to Madonna for me.

Sept 10, 1992

I had a dream that the Wayans brothers wanted to kick my ass. Shawn Wayans sprayed blue toilet bowl cleaner in my face.

Oct 4, 1992

Last night in my dream, I was hanging out with Madonna at the Waldorf Astoria in New York. It had a hole in the floor that you could fall through forever. She said, "Sleep with me or go down the hole."

Oct 24, 1992

I had a dream that Daniel Day Lewis was a stand-up comic, but nobody knew. He was a great actor who was also funny! He was handsome too.

Dec 4, 1992

I had a dream last night that Arnold Schwarzenegger was picking me up and throwing me around, but when I looked up at him he had a huge cut in his pectoral, not bloody, just deep. He said "Don't worry it isn't real," and he took off his whole torso and it revealed a much smaller torso. Then he just stood there, kind of frail like. I felt sad for him.

Dec 12, 1992

I dreamt I was with Geena Davis and we were taking LSD. Then we got naked. At first she didnt want to have sex, but then she let me put my finger in her. She said "Just a little" then I lost a lot of my hair. It was burnt off by the drug. Then she started hanging out with Kate Pierson of the B-52's.

9.

JK in the UK

> *English? Who needs that?*
> *I'm never going to England.*
> —Homer Simpson

As I neared the end of my last year at Baron/Brown, I decided to audition for a program at the British Academy of Dramatic Arts. I thought that just saying the words of Shakespeare and letting them roll off my tongue was going to make me a better, more well-rounded actor. It was the most difficult dialogue in existence. I felt that, if could break it down and understand it, I could do anything. I was expecting an amazing experience.

I auditioned and was accepted, with a partial scholarship. I needed to raise over $2000 to go. I hit up everyone I knew, but I barely raised anything. I had read in some book that celebrities always reacted to sob stories. So I decided to start writing to famous actors, asking them for money. I wrote to Kenneth Branagh, Carrie Fisher, and Don Henley, among others. The funny thing is that all my letters sounded pretty much the same—completely insincere. In fact, if someone wrote *me* these letters now, I wouldn't answer them. My reasoning for writing to these particular celebrities was ludicrous. Like, I wrote to Don Henley because he was a big supporter of Walden Woods. And I guess I thought a rainforest was essentially the same thing as me. My letter to Carrie Fisher was completely insane. The strange thing about it is that I ended up working with Carrie Fisher's sister Joely two years later, on *Ellen*. Also, I wrote a letter to Steve Martin, and I ended up working with him, too. Coincidence? I don't think so. It was the celebrity-letter-writing campaign!

Actually, the campaign was a total bust. No one sent me a dime. I raised about $300 by putting together a comedy show and charging ten bucks a head. My brother and my aunt gave me $600 each. Then, my parents saw the effort I was making and fronted me the rest. If it wasn't for them, I wouldn't have made it.

Here are the letters. Analyze as you see fit:

Elizabeth Peters
Silver Spring, MD

Dear Aunt Elizabeth:

This is your nephew Jamie writing. I am
asking for your help. I have been accepted into
a well-known acting program in Oxford,
England, to study Shakespeare. The experience
will help me pursue my dream of becoming an
actor. However, the cost of the tuition and living
expenses is very high and I cannot do it alone.
That is why I turn to you.

With your help, I can get there. If you could
spare just a small donation like $75 or $100 or
loan that I will gladly pay back within two
years.

We are related by blood so thick no one can
separate it.

Enclosed are two letters of recommendation
from my two teachers to the Dean of Admission
of the school. I enclosed them so you can see
that they believe in me. I hope you don't mind
me writing to you out of the blue like this. It's
just that I'm trying every possible way to
achieve my goal.

Yours sincerely,
Your nephew,
Jamie Kennedy

Don Henley
West Hollywood, CA

Dear Mr. Henley,

My name is Jamie Kennedy. I am a young
artist studying to become an actor. In the last
month I have auditioned for and been accepted
to a school in Oxford, England to study
Shakespeare. Wow.

It is a chance of a lifetime and after the school's
partial scholarship and my own savings, I'm
still short $2250 for airfare and remaining
tuition. I know you are a very charitable man
and I am not asking for that amount by any
means. I understand what you did with Walden
Woods, and although I'm not dying of cancer or
anything as severe as AIDS, this is still a dream
of mine, and I'm trying everything I can to
achieve it.

I think that through my art the world can
become a better place, if I can just open up one
person's mind.

Although at this point in my life money is low,
I will gladly donate my time and energy before
I leave and after I return to one or more of
your favorite charities, in the way you see fit. I
know you must get a thousand letters like this,
so if you disregard it, I will understand. Thank
you for your time.

Jamie Kennedy

By the time I got to Carrie Fisher's letter, I was desperate. So I decided to take another tack.

Carrie Fisher
Hollywood, CA

Dear Ms. Fisher,

Hello. My name is Jamie Kennedy. I am a young artist studying to be an actor. On May 12, I auditioned for a school in Oxford called the British American Drama Academy.

Three days later, I found out that I was accepted. I was elated. It is a once in a lifetime chance.

The thing is, although the school gave me a partial scholarship, I am still short $2250 for airfare and remaining tuition. I am not asking for all that, just a sum that you see fit.

By the way, I have lupus.

Your friend,

Jamie Kennedy

A week before I graduated from Baron/Brown and left for Oxford, I got kicked out of my apartment. At that time, I was memorizing my scenes in *The Iceman Cometh*, which was to be my last scene for acting class. We were taught in school that you could never be too prepared, so I was compulsive about rehearsing, going over line after line, from about eleven at night until four or five in the morning. Every time I successfully finished delivering a line, I would swing a golf club at a balled up sock. It was my little ritual.

After about a week of this, I finally got to the last page. I started going crazy, smacking the sock with the golf club. "I'm done! I'm done!" I yelled. It was three-thirty in the morning.

Out of nowhere—BLLLAAAAHHHHHBOOM! The loudest crash I'd ever heard in my life, coming from the downstairs apartment. It sounded like a war zone. Then, my downstairs neighbor shouted, "MOTHERFUCKER! You've done it! You've finally done it! You've made noise for the last time! You hear me? You're dead! Where's my axe?"

I began pleading through the floorboards, "I'm sorry! I'm sorry!"

"Too bad!" he screamed, and started bounding up the stairs. In a state of total fright, I climbed out my window, dropped from the ledge and ran like hell. I slept in my car that night. The next day, I snuck in, left my neighbor an apologetic note, and moved all my stuff out of the apartment. I never went back.

I loaded up all my belongings into the car and parked it in this secret spot right behind the Scientology Building, where, at that time, you would never get ticketed. (They control everything!) I had nowhere to put the car while I was in England, so when I took off three days later, I just left it on the street, hoping for the best.

———

Although I was able to scrape together enough money to attend the program, I couldn't afford the school's lodging or the meal plan. I found a really cheap place to live off-campus, a room above a thirteenth century blacksmith shop. In order to eat, I had to sneak into the school's cafeteria and snag whatever food I could before I got caught.

I attempted to go incognito by wearing a big winter jacket with a hood that covered my face. I'm not quite sure why I thought my disguise would make me inconspicuous, since it was the middle of summer and everyone else was in shorts and tank tops. I was like a giant vagrant in the middle of this stately room. The discrepancy was ridiculous—I looked like a homeless bum and everyone else looked like they were in a Gap ad.

Whether or not I ended up eating depended on who was serving food. The cook generally refused me, but the lunch lady felt sorry for me. Usually, she'd hand me some cheese or potatoes and say, "There you go, luv. Take that and put it in your gullet," sounding exactly like one of Monty Python's cleaning lady characters. I'd run out of the cafeteria and eat the food in the bushes.

―――――

In our first week at BADA, we had to audition to be placed on a certain track. Track one was super stars, track two was intermediate, and track three was remedial acting. All we lacked was a kid-with-Down's-Syndrome track. I was put on track two.

My paperwork must have somehow gotten screwed up. I had to jump through more hoops and reaudition to be placed in a specific group within track two. The audition consisted of a reading in front of fifty track two students. I picked a passage from *Othello*. While I was in the middle of my reading, I remembered how Laurence Olivier said that when doing

Shakespeare, you should move around a lot. I decided to take his advice. First, I climbed on top of a piano and began to dance around. Then, I jumped off the piano and started running around the room. I got right in people's faces and shouted my lines. Finally, I hopped up and down and sang a few of my lines opera-style, "It is the cause, it is the cause, my soul. Let me not name it to you, you chaste stars!"

I felt *great*. Then, Linda, the woman in charge of the program, asked me to step outside. She took a huge breath, looked deep into my eyes and said, "Okay. The drugs have to go, or I'm going to ask you to leave."

I was dumbfounded. "What are you talking about?" I never did drugs and I barely ever drank. I didn't want anything to break my career focus.

"You know," she said confidently. "The drugs. Your audition? You were all over the place. Who shouts? Who jumps up and down? Who?"

"Excuse me," I interrupted, "I thought this was an ACTING CLASS. You're supposed to go nuts!"

She squinted at me. I started to get angry. "Give me a piece of litmus paper and I'll piss on it," I shouted. I'm sure that quelled her fears. "I don't do drugs! Let me piss!"

"We don't have any urine tests here," she said.

"Go ask somebody then," I said, pulling her back into the classroom. I shouted to my classmates, "Am I on drugs?"

Most of them didn't know me, but a couple of girls shouted out, "No, you're just weird."

The whole school heard about this. Then, a few days later, I was eating my stolen lunch in the bushes. Linda walked by and spotted me. She called out over the shrubbery, "Oh hi, Jamie. Constance told me you're not on drugs. Sorry." Then she walked away, as if nothing had ever happened. Like she needed to hear it from some Sigma Delta Chi? She couldn't just take my fucking word for it? Was it because I ate in the bushes?!

After a little while, the teachers forgot about the drug incident. There shouldn't have been an incident in the first place, but Linda had gone around telling the whole faculty I was a fucking speed freak. I was fuming. I mean, all the other students in the program were these rich college kids who would go home after class and get high every day. But they just sat there in acting class, stoned and quiet, so no one thought twice about them. Here I was, completely drug free, actually trying to learn *acting*—and I was the suspect.

———

The place was bullocks (British for bullshit!). I was expecting an intense acting school, regimented like a Russian gymnastics academy, with a rigorous work ethic and a lot of discipline. But it lacked serious commitment from the other students. It was like a rich kids" playground—a cool European summer vacation on Daddy's dime. I found out that even the audition had been bogus. Anyone could get in. It was all about the money. The students didn't want to be actors. They wanted to be cool. They were happy to spend every day just talking endlessly about acting theory and method and smoking clove cigarettes.

Alan Rickman came to speak to our class one day. He said, "Acting is just child's play. It's really nothing. Nothing. Questions?"

The students started coming up with these pompous questions, trying to showcase their intelligence. "How do you think the theater of the absurd works against the theater of conceit?" "Isn't it possible that *Titus Andronicus*'s anti-oedipal violence stemmed from the societal obligations of paternity?" "Do you agree with Kafka's interpretation of Czech puppetry as a fiercely cabalistic blend of commerce and mysticism?"

I couldn't believe the questions these potheads were asking. Meanwhile, I had real, practical things to ask Alan Rickman. I raised my hand. "Yessssssss?" said Rickman.

"Mr. Rickman," I began, "I just wanted to let you know that I'm a big fan of your work."

"Another foooooooooooooool," he droned.

I began my questions. "Uh. . . . What was it like to work with Bruce Willis in *Die Hard*? Was he cool? I heard he was." My classmates looked at me with scorn.

"Well, I'd just finished a twenty-week run of *Dangerous Liaisons* on Broadway, so it was like a vacation," Rickman answered slowly. "It was kind of like playing a carrrtooooooon character."

"Thanks," I said.

Rickman started to call on the next person. "And what's it like to be famous?" I blurted out.

He replied, "The limousines get longer and the windows get blacker. Neeeeeeexxxxxxxxxxtttt!"

Everyone just shook their head at me. The weirdo was acting up again. That was basically a template for my whole Oxford experience. I was the weird guy, the odd man out. I was the guy who didn't drink Guinness—or anything else for that matter; the guy who lived off campus above the shoe cobbler; the guy who didn't smoke pot; the guy who didn't want to start a theater group; the guy whose clothes weren't right; the guy who was constipated from all the stolen cheese. I was that guy and I hated it. But I didn't just hate myself. I hated them, too.

I also hated Judi Dench! When she spoke to our class, I asked her, "How can I work in England? Like, can I work with the Royal Shakespeare Company?"

She paused, then said, "Ha ha ha ha! Darling, it's impossible for you to work in England. You're an A-merican. You don't *have* your green card."

"Well, what if I worked to get it?" I asked.

"Ha ha ha ha. . . . *Darling!*" she smirked. "You should just stick to A-merica."

I thought to myself, "Well, then you can't come over to our country and do *Wings*, bitch."

After four weeks, I got on a plane home, thrilled to be getting out of England. I'd always heard how wonderful Oxford was. Oxford is so quaint, what a sense of history, Bill Clinton studied at Oxford. Oxford this, Oxford that, Oxford, Oxford, Oxford. And you know what? The food sucked, the people were drunks, the town was decrepit, the phones were rotary, the toilets didn't flush, and everyone took off two hours to drink tea in the afternoon. And you couldn't get a vegetable to save your life.

LA may have had its issues, but at least it wasn't snobbish. It was plastic and phony and shallow, but it knew its place. LA said, "Yeah my tits are fake! Didn't my doctor do a good job?"

I couldn't wait to get back there and be homeless again. And when I returned, my car was untouched, without even a single ticket.

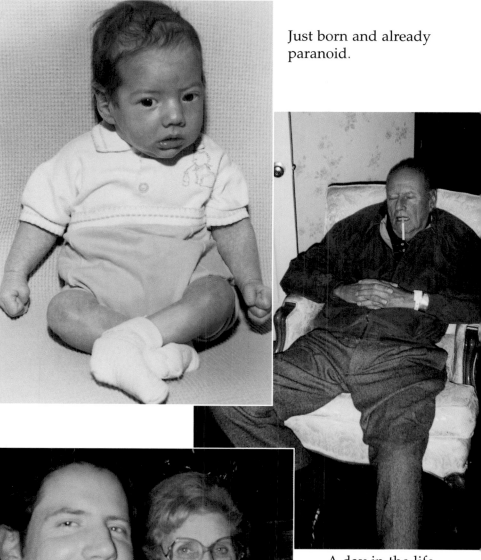

Just born and already
paranoid.

A day in the life
of Bob Kennedy:
"Ah say, sir,
ah say . . . zzz."

Mackin' on Mom.

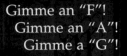

Gimme an "F"!
Gimme an "A"!
Gimme a "G"!

Crap, what page is "Our Father" on?
(*I am second from left*)

A gentle lover
of animals.

Making up
for my wussy
childhood
by auditioning
for *American
History X.*

How did I go from this . . .

. . . to this?
Where did it all
go wrong?

Twelve years old—
skippety doodee!

Upper Darby
love—I picked
her up on my
unicycle.

My Indian phase.

Ritchie Cunningham . . .
in Crackville.

Hello, my name is Jamie Earth. Put your toe on my heart.

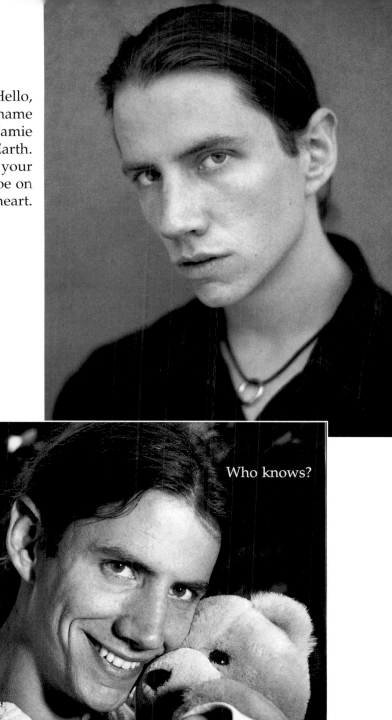

Who knows?

Fresh from the tanning salon—welcome to my crib.

Me hating my life while making a bunny . . . or is it a giraffe?
Oh, fuck it.

SHORT NOVEL! DEMISE OF ARLENE

NATIONAL
LAMPOON

REE!
GIOUS
WYER
AZINE

MERICAN
ORKMANSHIP:
LL IT'S CRACKED
P TO BE?

ILD THINGS:
OU'VE GOT
O SEE IT
O BELIEVE IT!

EVIL'S
DVOCATE:
WORKING
ANUAL
OR WHITEY

U.S. $3.95 CANADA $4.9.
JAPAN Intense Yen

My first cover. I thought it was tasteful; my mother thought
it was porn.

Getting ready to cruise Santa Monica Boulevard? No, it's just my wardrobe test for *As Good As It Gets*.

My morning ritual.

Got blood? Freshly killed in *Scream 2*.

The man who made me want to be an actor—the King.

Asking Michael Caine about *Zulu*.

Ice Cube throwin' Westside signs at me.

Mark Wahlberg throwin' Westside signs at me.

George Clooney throwin' water at me.

If David Crosby
and Frank Zappa
had a baby.

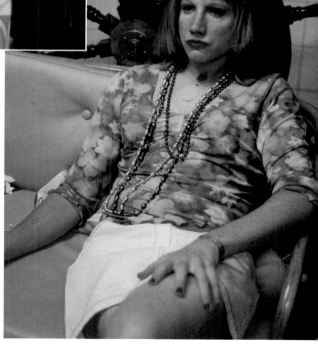

My childhood
cross-dressing
finally pays off
on *JKX*.

My first marriage—
I think I make a
nice June bride.

I see you!!!

Come to bed, baby . . .

Don't let me catch your ass at Gymboree, bee-yatch!

My bedroom scene in *Malibu's Most Wanted*— one Oreo cookie comin' up.

My life is ridiculous.

10.

The Power of Marty

A lie told often enough becomes the truth.
—Vladimir Ilyich Lenin

What's Happening to Us?

After I came back from Oxford, I spent three weeks sleeping in my car. By "sleeping," I mean staying awake in a paranoid frenzy, trying to determine whether the loud noises I'd just heard were gunshots. It was really frightening. I always thought someone was going to reach in and grab me. Or gang bangers were going to jack my car with me in it, and use it for a drive-by.

One open mic night at Royal Grounds coffee shop, I ran into Ernie Griffin, a forty-eight-year-old standup comedian who I knew from the comedy circuit. Ernie was a nice man, but odd—he had this nasal New York accent that made him sound exactly like the devil in *The Exorcist* when he said the line, "Spare some change for an old altar boy, father?" I told Ernie about my living situation and he said, "Hey, why don't you

```
Aug 22, 1993

CAR Goals  Things to do to get out of my car.

1) Get job
2) Get place
3) Get phone
4) Get answering machine
5) Get refridgerator
6) Get futon
7) Get agent
```

move in with me? I'm squatting in this empty apartment. No one knows I'm there."

Under normal circumstances, I would have had some definite reservations about living with a stranger. But I had nowhere to go, so I jumped at the offer.

Ernie immediately began to showcase his eccentricities. He walked around the apartment reciting obscure facts—all day, every day. "Did you hear? President Clinton got athlete's foot. Yeah, he caught it in the Truman Sauna Room."

"You know that John Denver's song 'Rocky Mountain High' was about his fear of heights? Yeah, he's got vertigo."

"Herbie Hancock had an enema. Yeah, apparently he's got hemorrhoids. I'm going to the bathroom. You need anything?"

Every time I walked into the apartment, I found Ernie in the corner, eating government-issue canned pork. He had somehow gotten hooked up with Social Services. They provided him with a regular supply of food stamps, which he used to purchase the pork and also canned peaches—those were his two treats. He claimed to be standing in the corner because he needed sunlight. Later, I found out that Ernie hid his non-government-issue crack cocaine under a loose floorboard in the corner. So he was eating peaches as an appetizer, pork as a meal, and smoking crack for desert. Talk about a well-balanced meal—he was in the zone.

Ernie dated a girl named Frankie, who he suspected of being a man. "She only lets me do her from behind and she won't let me touch her front," he said. "And she's got a little bit of goatee stubble."

"So is she a woman?" I asked.

"I don't know," he said.

"Well when you have sex with her, do you feel a vulva or a sphincter? Or is it just some skin flaps?"

"I don't know."

"Why don't you ask her if she has a penis?"

"I sort of don't want to know," he said.

"Do you love her?" I asked

"Kinda. Plus she makes an amazing turkey chili burrito with chipotle sauce."

"Then just wear a bag," I said.

———

The squat was actually in a very nice building. The only reason Ernie knew about it was because another comic named Kyle had a condo there. We had free gas and running water. And Kyle was always supportive, telling me, "Hang in there. One day you'll have enough money to buy this whole place."

My mother came through and visited me in LA for two days. We had no electricity, so she brought me a battery powered lamp. She looked around and said, "It's better than some of the other places you've lived in." Then she pointed to my skateboard and asked, "Is that your car?"

The biggest problem with the apartment was that we

didn't have a phone line. Luckily, Ernie wasn't just a sexually confused, crack-smoking joke spinner, but also a crafty former Pacific Bell technician. One night at three A.M., Ernie scaled our neighbor's telephone pole and connected our unused wires into their already active phone line. Just like that, we had a live phone line and free service, twenty-four hours a day. All we had to do was pick up the phone and make sure the line was clear. If so, we were in good shape. Aside from being felons, that is.

The byproduct of this situation was that we had the unfettered ability to hear our neighbors' conversations. One day, I came home to find Ernie crouched over the phone, a mesmerized expression on his face.

"What are you doing?" I asked.

"Shhhh!" he whispered. "I'm listening to this guy, Gary. He's a recovering alcoholic who just started a band! I think they're called Alvin and the Fuckmunks, but I'm not sure. A garbage truck drove by and I couldn't hear."

"Dude, that's just wrong," I said. "Hang up."

"No way," Ernie said. "Gary's about to convince his girl-friend Jennifer to have a three-way with her hot downstairs neighbor."

I yanked the phone out of his hand and put it up to my ear. For the next two hours, I listened to Gary and Jennifer argue. Despite myself, I was fascinated. It was like getting a glimpse into these strangers' souls.

Before long, Ernie and I were addicted to other people's lives. We'd hang out in our apartment every day, share Ernie's canned peaches minus the crack, and listen to strangers talk about their most intimate moments. It got so I never wanted to leave.

One day, I had to go out for a few hours. I came home and grilled Ernie. "What'd Gary do today?" I asked.

"Gary got Jennifer pregnant!" he told me. "Gary's freaking out—he wants her to have an abortion, but he doesn't want to pay for it. Jennifer's mom won't give her the money because she thinks Jennifer's on drugs. Gary's pretty torn up about the whole thing. He's started drinking again."

"Well, he should have thought about the consequences before he stuck it in!"

I couldn't believe how Gary was acting. Feeling indignant, I convinced Ernie that we needed to confront him. We found out where Gary lived by following the phone wire from our building to our shared telephone pole to his apartment building. Then, we went back to our place, listened to Gary's phone calls and waited. A few hours later, Gary got off the phone to do some laundry. We had our opening. Ernie and I ran back to Gary's building and started hitting random numbers on the intercom. Some stranger buzzed us in. We crept into the laundry room to find a short, nerdy-looking guy stuffing tighty whiteys into a dryer.

"Gary? Is that you?" Ernie asked.

The guy turned around. "Yeah, I'm Gary. Do I know you?" he said.

Ernie and I looked at each other. We hadn't discussed what to do at this point. "No, uh, but I saw your band once," Ernie said, then turned to me expectantly.

I chickened out too. "Uh, yeah, you guys were really great. Fuckmunks rule!" Ernie nodded emphatically.

"Uh, thanks," Gary said, and went back to his laundry.

We turned and ran out.

———

After a few weeks, I got a part in a play called *Home Free*. I had nightly rehearsals, often running past the midnight hour. I came home exhausted, to find a morose Ernie pouting in the living room. "Where have you been?" he demanded. "I've been waiting for you all night!"

I tried to explain that I had to work around the clock, but Ernie only got more upset. "You don't even care about Gary anymore," he lamented. "What's *happening* to us?!"

Then, Ernie just stopped speaking to me. Every night, I asked him, "Hey Ernie. How was your day?" Every night, I got nothing but a cold shoulder. I tried to reestablish our relationship by including him in my life. "Ernie, you want to run lines with me?" I began.

He just said, "Hey, Kirby Pucket is allergic to chocolate. Yeah, he eats carob instead."

"It would really help me out," I continued.

"If Carter gets MVP, I'll shit a pickle."

"I don't know what you're talking about."

"Well, that's because you're a fucking faggot."

Clearly, he was lashing out. I didn't know what to do. He was really hurt. Our relationship needed to change . . . but how do you break up with a friend?

"I'm really sorry," I said. "I know I haven't been spending as much time with you as before. But this play is a big break for me."

"It's okay. I'm sorry too," he said, shuffling his feet. "You wanna go for some chalupas?"

I think that's what Farrah Fawcett's husband said to her in *The Burning Bed*.

Eventually, the situation resolved itself. Ernie left me to move in with Frankie and a couple of her/his girl/boyfriends. He said he needed his space.

———

Home Free

This show is a scream – and I don't mean funny. It's one long, shrill scream by performers who mistake yelling for acting and a director who never reins them in during the longest sixty-five-minute play an audience has ever had the misfortune to sit through. Lanford Wilson would be appalled at the mediocrity of this production of his stirring fantasy.

Jamie Kennedy and Judith Shelton are Lawrence and Joanna, a dim-witted brother-and-sister team who stare a tiny, grubby apartment – and a bed, much to the dismay of their landlord. Their nicknames could be "the incredibly Awful Whiners and Stompers" since that is the essence of both Kennedy's and Shelton's performances. Neither manages to convey the poignancy of their dilemma, and as a consequence, the audience is left with absolutely nothing to empathize with or care about. Joanna's pregnancy, the key to Wilson's clever show, becomes meaningless.

Director D.W. Brown began by miscasting the roles, then makes things worse by relinquishing control to these overzealous actors. The result: a torturous night at the theater.

• Gardner Stage, 1501 Gardner Street, Hollywood. (213) 654-3179. Fris-Sats at 8, Suns at 7.

Dec 25, 1993 (Xmas Goals)
Goals for 1994:

1) Get on stage at least once a night!
2) Always Know what I'm going on stage to do.
3) Never bring paper up on stage with me.
4) Do more Impressions on stage.
5) Don't whine on Stage.
6) Hump things.
7) Don't Mumble!!!
8) Eat 3 meals everyday.

(Note to reader: You may be wondering what number six is all about. I heard that Rob Schneider had gotten the lead in *Surf Ninjas* after going up on stage and humping things. I thought this could be a useful strategy.)

Despite his love of pork, Ernie was a very funny guy. He had a good comic mind and a great way of wrapping his head around a premise (and a transvestite). Without Ernie around, the apartment was quiet and depressing. I spent my first Christmas alone there. It was miserable. It was a rare rainy day in LA and everything was closed, so I couldn't do anything except sit in solitude. I went to see *Schindler's List* by myself and cried like a baby. Then, I came home and wrote out a list of goals for the year. God, it was so lonely. But I had to do it. My parents wanted me to come home, but I couldn't go, because I had nothing to show for my four and a half years in Los Angeles. I couldn't handle the well-meaning questions. I couldn't tell people that I lived without electricity, that my dinner every night was a tub of brown rice I bought at a Thai restaurant for $1.32. I didn't have enough money to go out in LA, so I just sat in my squat alone all week, doing push-ups and reading books, emerging only at night for open mics.

I was just sad. I had all this training, but nothing to do with it. I was going nowhere. I needed to find a way to move forward.

Small Potatoes

Knowing how down I was about my career, Kyle referred me to his commercial agents—Fred Carver, Inc. When I went up there for my first meeting, I learned The Great Hollywood Lesson— never talk shit about anyone else in public. I was in the elevator and some old guy got in. He said, "Where are you going?"

I said, "Fred Carver's Agency."

"Are they thinking about representing you?" he asked.

"I hope so," I said.

"I hear they're good."

I was about to answer, "Really? I hear they're old and lazy, but what else do I got, right?" As I was opening my mouth to speak, the elevator doors sprung open and an assistant ran up, panting, "Mr. Carver, Don needs you on line two, it's an emergency." I quickly shut the hell up.

Fred Carver ended up signing me. Then they began to exhibit severe finger-lifting issues. I think they sent me out once. The whole thing was a waste of time.

I then met with D.W. Brown, my acting teacher from Baron/Brown studio, to discuss my non-career. D.W. and his wife referred me to a manager named Howard Gross. I had to audition for him at his guest house, up Sunset Plaza Drive. When I first met him, he reminded me of a giggling Scooby Doo on speed. At any minute, he might come unhinged and just start shouting, "Ahhhhhheeheeheehee!" He always had this look on his face that seemed to me a combination of, "I'm gay, I'm on coke, I'm in Hollywood, I'm horny, but I may want to represent you." It never changed. But he was smart. And when he got on the phone, he screamed like a mad man. He was a gay tornado.

He wanted me to come up with an audition using material by David Mamet or Sam Shepherd. I practiced my scene from *American Buffalo* over and over, just walking around my apartment, saying "Fucking Ruthie" for hours. After I did my little speech for Howard, he said, "That's good. Now try this *SeaQuest* copy." *SeaQuest* was a series on NBC that starred Roy Scheider as a marine biologist who had a special relationship with the sea and all the creatures in it. He also fought monsters every week. I guess Howard wanted to make sure I had range.

After I finished my *SeaQuest* performance, Howard said, "Ooooh, I want to put you in my hip pocket."

"What?"

Howard explained: hip-pocketing meant he was taking me on with little commitment—"Don't expect too much." He'd call me when he had something for me, but I couldn't demand anything of him. It was like dating, but still being allowed to see other people. Ahhhhhheeheeheehee!

Howard sent me out on two auditions. One was a live movie version of *Beavis and Butthead*. I went back a couple of times, but then they decided to make it as a cartoon. The other was a pilot—a spin-off of *Mighty Morphin Power Rangers* called *Cybertron*. That one I booked.

The characters I read for were guys named Elmo and Cleetus who were like Beavis and Butthead. (Theme!) Beavis and Butthead were huge at the time, so whenever anyone was casting two goofy sidekicks, that was the model. I had to go through seven auditions. After the third, I got partnered up with this guy named Robin, who was a student at USC. I think they only liked us because we both had really long hair. Mine was long because I was too broke to get it cut, and I was also finding myself. His was long because he was a dirtball.

During our first rehearsal, I made the mistake of giving Robin what I thought were helpful notes on his performance, saying, "You know what might be funny? Instead of going, 'Hey, *dude*,' you could try putting the accent on the hey. Like, '*Heyyyy*, dude.'"

Robin's face got bright red. He glared at me and said, "You're not the comedy god."

"I was just trying to help," I said.

"I . . . I . . . hate you!" he shrieked. Then he stamped his foot and stormed out of the room.

On the *seventh* audition, we went in and met with the executive producer, Haim Saban. He kept saying stuff like, "How do you see the character's arc?" The whole time I was just thinking, "Dude, I live in a squat. His arc is to get me electricity." When we were waiting in the lobby, I saw, like, six other potential Beavis and Buttheads. All the bad buddy-comedy clichés were in full effect—there was the black guy/white guy team, the short/tall guys, and the fat/skinny duo. For some reason, they went with us, the two Pearl Jam rejects.

It was so hard for me to get to the auditions because my car was on its last legs. I had to bum rides or take the bus. The day before we shot the pilot, my car finally died. I was so scared that I was going to be late that I took the earliest bus I could get on. I arrived at four A.M. for an eight A.M. call. I just stood outside and said my lines over and over again.

The job was a nightmare. Everyone hated us. At one point during the shoot, the network sent the two actors who were the *Power Rangers* version of us (they were a tall/short combo) over to our set, to give us pointers on how to make our scenes funnier. They said, "You guys should fall down a lot while hitting each other and stuff." I was in hell. The only way to make it funny would have been to stop shooting altogether and burn the set down. Now *that* would have been hilarious.

Everybody got fired from the project except the lead. Howard stopped calling me back. It didn't matter. A few weeks back, I was in Howard's office looking through a copy of *Variety*, one of the entertainment industry's two trade papers. He gestured to *Variety* and said, "If you get your name in that paper, then you've hit the big time. You won't need me anymore." It's a statement that has stuck with me for ten years. From then on in, I knew the guy was small potatoes. I mean, I already thought he was gay potatoes. And I thought he was coke potatoes. But I figured that at least he was good phone potatoes. Now I knew he was just tater tots.

The Top Booker in this Bitch

I was able to stay in my squat for five months because a bank had foreclosed on the apartment. They couldn't sell it until they resolved the outstanding legal issues. One day, a real estate broker came to show the apartment and realized that someone was living there. I ran outside and waited. The broker came out with a befuddled look on her face. Her clients were just standing around, not knowing what to do. After they left, Kyle came out and said, "Dude, she's gonna call the Sheriff." I went in and got my stuff. Then I went back to living in my car. This time it was a Mustang I'd bought off my friend Barry—he was letting me pay it off fifty bucks at a time. It was way too small for me, but it had a bucket seat—now I was cooking with gas! I couldn't take it anymore, though.

A comedian named Dave Garrett came to my rescue. Dave was a lawyer and did the deals for all of our open mic-ers. Like if we had a gig in Pacomia, he would make sure we got a meal *and* gas money. Dave was a monster negotiator, and cunning, too. He had somehow convinced *National Lampoon* to let him run their magazine. For one issue, he put a picture of me on the cover, dressed as a plumber, complete with ass crack. When I showed it to my mother, she said, "You're in porn."

Dave was living with Penelope, a forty-five-year-old woman with sons our age. He offered to rent me her garage. I moved in on the day of the Northridge earthquake.

Penelope's garage was the best place I had lived in to date. But there was one small hitch—I had to pay rent. Barry told me that he had a great job working at a telemarketing agency, selling toner. "What's toner?" I asked.

He said, "Just come down and meet my boss."

Barry's boss, Burt, was a total throwback to the fifties—one of those rockabilly dudes with full sleeves of tattoos on their arms and Elvis hair. He parked his motorcycle in the middle of the office. Burt didn't have much of a screening process. He asked, "Do you have a driver's license?"

"Yeah," I said.

"And a Social Security card?"

"Yeah."

"Congratulations," he said. "You're hired."

"Great," I said. "What's toner?"

"Just come in tomorrow."

I researched, discovered that toner was the name of ink cartridges used in printers and photocopiers, and decided to go for it. The place was in the basement of an apartment building on La Brea, two doors down from the Seventh Veil strip club—right in the heart of Hollywood. The people who worked there were struggling musicians, wannabe actors, drug addicts, motorheads, homeless people (me), blacks, whites, Asians, welfare moms, and a couple of horny old men. Anybody who was trying to make a quick buck. Despite the lax interview, Burt turned out to be a strict disciplinarian, running the place like an army sergeant. He had been in the marines for four years (before he got the tattoos). We had to be in exactly at six A.M. to call people on the east coast who started work at nine A.M. If we were late, we got a slip. Three slips and we were gone. He gave everybody a chance to work, but he needed his room to be tight.

Burt started me out on model numbers. This entailed calling a bunch of companies from a list of leads acquired by other telemarketers. Once I got someone on the phone, I would ask them for the model number of the photocopier in their office.

When I secured the model number, I would turn it over to our salesman. He would use the number to figure out what kind of toner the office's copier used. Then, he would call back and pose as the company's usual copier salesman or copier repair guy, and say, "Hey, there's been a price increase in the toner. We've gone from $290 to $298 a carton. We'll fax you a verification form. Just sign it and fax it back." Then, he'd fax them a sales order, which they'd usually sign without even reading. So, our agency would bill them almost $300 for the same toner they could get at Staples for forty bucks. Usually the company was so large that no one ever noticed. It was technically legal, but really shady.

There was a standardized procedure in place for all the phone calls. We used a script that outlined opening statements, possible objections that people might make and our responses to those objections. If someone refused to give out a model number three times, we were supposed hang up, because they probably weren't going to bite.

Burt instructed me in the fine art of picking a phone name. Jamie Kennedy sounded too Irish Catholic.

"See, if you call someone who hates micks, you're screwed. You need something blander."

"Like what?" I said.

"I like to use inanimate objects," he said. "People really can't figure that out. Why don't you be Tom Ruglin? Because, what nationality is a rug?"

I thought, *Persian*?

————

When I first started working there, I didn't know what the salesmen did with the numbers. So I didn't think working there was that bad—just another low-rent job. Soon enough though, I realized what was going on.

I thought I could deal with it. But this was right around the time that I started getting into free yoga classes, because it was the only exercise regime I could afford. Every day, I would wake up at three-forty-five A.M. to take a free four A.M. class at the Seik Center. At five in the morning, I'd be stretching into a downward facing dog.

"Breathe in the blue air and breathe out the green," my yoga teacher would say, aligning my spine. I'd inhale and exhale, feeling peaceful and whole.

An hour later, I'd be bilking unsuspecting Iowa secretaries out of their companies' money. I started feeling like my chakras were deceptive.

I tried to talk to my fellow employees about this, but they weren't having any part of it. "Don't neg vibe me," they'd say.

"This whole place is a neg vibe," I'd say. "Don't you feel bad, just lying to people all day?"

"I don't lie," they'd answer, defensively. "Everything I do is in accordance with proper telemarketing procedure."

"Well, how about when you call people and say you're from Xerox Customer Service?" I'd ask.

"No, I say I'm calling *with* Xerox. That means I'm calling with the Xerox photocopier right next to me," they'd reply. "It's all about the prepositions you use."

"What about when you say that the new price of toner is $386? They sell that stuff at Office Depot for forty bucks!"

"These *are* the prices," they'd protest. "My prices."

"What about the fake name you use on the phone?" I'd say, totally frustrated at this point.

"It's not a fake name," they'd scoff. "It's a nickname."

When all else failed, they would try to justify it with some form of warped logic. "Do you think a pizza costs $12?" they'd ask. "Fuck no. A pizza costs sixty cents. The cheese is forty-five cents, the sauce is a dime, and the dough is a nickel. They fucking jack that shit up and the working man gets fucked. Who am I fucking here? IBM? Fuck IBM! They're Nazis! I'm just getting mine!"

I felt dirty.

Despite having huge qualms about the place, I stayed on. I needed the money. I got paid seventy cents for every model number I obtained. At first, I figured I could get a hundred numbers a day to make seventy bucks. How hard could it be? HARD. I was a terrible salesman. I'd get to work at six A.M. and by 6:04 ladies would be telling me to go to hell. I mean, I wouldn't have eaten my bagel yet, and already I'd have to go to hell. Once, this woman went ballistic on me, telling me to "stick my own finger up my ass." But there was something about the way she insulted me that was really sexy and a big turn on. She was so strong and had such a potty mouth.

After she slammed down the phone, I called her back. I said, "Hi, it's me again. I just talked to you a second ago. Please don't hang up. See, when you slammed the phone down, there was just something in it that really turned me on." I paused, but she didn't speak. I continued, "Do you think you could do it again?"

"Well, you're a sick little pervert, aren't you?" she said.

"Yeah," I said.

"You'd probably like it if I called you a cocksucker too," she said.

"Uh huh," I said.

"Go to hell, you fucking maggot," she said, slamming down the phone again. I called back. This time I got her voicemail. "Hi, this is Wendy," she chirped. "I've stepped away from my desk for a moment. Please leave a message and I'll call you back. Unless you're that goddamn mother-fucking phone scum who keeps stalking me. Fuck you and your fucking father, you fucking dick face!" Goddamn, she was hot.

The job depressed me. I couldn't even concentrate on the work—it was just so soul-sucking and tedious. I spent all my time on the job goofing off, trying out new jokes and impersonations on my coworkers.

One day, Burt sat me down for a heart-to-heart. He said, "You screw around too much, Scumbag" (that was his pet name for everyone). "If you used one-third of your talent on the phone, you could be the top booker in this bitch."

"I don't want to be the top booker," I said.

"But you've got to make a living somehow, while you're trying to be an actor," he said. "Why not make the best of it?"

"I can't sell anything," I said. "I ask and they hang up."

"You're doing it all wrong," he said. "You don't ask, you assume. ASSUME THE SALE. Look, you're already giving it to them, whether they know it or not. And that's how you gotta treat it. Like you're just giving them a courtesy call."

"I'll try," I said, half-heartedly.

"Listen, Jamie," he said, totally intense. "You have a gift."

I was taken aback. "You think so?" I said.

"I mean it, man."

I hadn't gotten that much positive reinforcement in all my years in Hollywood. I was kind of flattered. The guy was such an incredible salesman that he sold me on myself.

I decided that he was right. As long as I had to have this job, I might as well make some money at it. The thing is, my voice was kind of goofy and childlike—often I'd call customers and they'd think I was a kid making crank calls. But I'd always been good at impersonating people. So I started using different voices to sell toner.

I'd call up, a woman would answer, and I'd coo into the phone, "Hiiiii, this is Marsha, calling about the copier!" If I were dialing a southern state, I called as Buck, using my best hillbilly drawl. If the guy answering the phone sounded gay,

I'd be an effeminate man named Leslie who made lots of references to Gucci. For Brooklyn calls, I was Vinnie da repairman. "Yeah, how you doin'?"

My sales doubled. Burt was happy. My career as a con artist was off to a fine start. Unfortunately, my career as an actor left a lot to be desired. And my career as a decent human being was in the toilet.

Then I had an epiphany. I had gained a new skill: the ability to sell anything. And I started thinking, *If I can sell this worthless toner, something that I don't even care about, why can't I sell something of value . . . like myself? After all, I might not be your typical leading man, but I have some good qualities and I'm at least as charismatic as toner.* I needed to look at myself as a product. I needed to sell myself, as if I were top of the line Canon LBP-HX/ color laser toner.

I needed to become my own agent.

Don't Get Greedy

I knew that I could easily do a better job of agenting than any agent or manager I'd ever had. I worked hard, I believed in myself, and now I knew how to sell anything. However, there was a little hitch in my plan. To truly become my own agent, I needed money for stuff like stationary, videotapes, and a phone line. To make money, I had to keep working. But as my own agent, I needed be available around the clock.

Then, I got a huge break. A comedienne named Sheryl Weingard, who worked at an ad agency, told me that her company was looking for five comedians to do a test spot for the El Pollo Loco fast food chain. A test spot is basically a sample commercial that the ad agency uses to sell the client an idea. The job paid $75—I was *in.*

I went to Orange County along with four other comedians

to test for the ad. This particular spot was called "Dr. Science Man." We wore white lab coats and took turns sitting at a desk in what looked like a doctor's office. Our only prop was a clear model of the male human body, the kind that shows all the internal organs. We had to improvise some material about the El Pollo Loco chicken and what eating it did to the human body. All I did was act like Jim Carrey, who I'd just seen in *Ace Ventura*. I became the body's individual parts—when the chicken went into the mouth, I played the part of the mouth, then the esophagus, then the stomach, and so on.

They picked my spot to show to their El Pollo Loco clients. The El Pollo Loco executives decided to go with a commercial that featured their mascot, a singing, dancing cartoon chicken, instead. How many jobs was I going to lose to these fucking evil cartoons? But the ad agency people liked me. They offered me a job doing the same kind of test spots for Vans sneakers. I got a raise—my salary was $200 and five pairs of sneakers. At the time, I only had one pair of sneakers—the same pair for working out, for dinner, for business. Now, five! I was finally moving up.

For the shoot, I went into the Vans factory and basically just goofed around. The ad agency cut together four little promo spots and showed them to the head of Vans. They said that if Vans liked them, I would get a chance to audition for the commercial. I thought this was great—an amazing break. Then I got a phone call from the ad people. The owner of Vans had watched the spots and said, "That's our guy."

It was amazing—I got paid $5500 for making four commercials. Before we started, I asked the ad agency for the two hundred bucks they still owed me. "Well, Jamie, since you got that commercial, we're going to waive that fee," they said. "Don't get greedy."

"Don't get greedy? We had a deal! I'm living in a garage," I wanted to say. Instead, I kept my mouth shut.

Despite the $200 shortfall, I still had enough money to set my plan in motion. Even more importantly, I had tape. And I could get my SAG card. I can't stress how crucial this is for struggling actors. When you're starting out, no agent or manager will even look at you without a SAG card or tape. It's like you're not a real actor to them. No agent wants to watch an actor do a scene in their office. Now I had the ability to say, "Here's some tape of me in a national commercial." If an agent sees that someone has hired you before, they think, *I have to have him before someone else does.*

With cash and tape in hand, I quit my job at the Toner Room, set up a little office in Penelope's garage, and devoted myself to becoming my own, full-time agent.

Make the Other Person Feel Important, But Do it Sincerely!

I knew that I couldn't just straight up "sell" myself—people would either think I was arrogant or certifiable. I had to use a fictional representative. For the past year, I had been doing a bit in my act about an agent named Marty. He was an amalgam of various people I'd met in Hollywood, including the owner of an agency to whom I used to deliver sandwiches. Also, I incorporated my former manager Steven Scheinbaum and his partner Mel Levine, who both had raspy smokers' voices.

I decided to test the waters. I called a guy named Vincent Marcel, a New York agent whose name I had just seen in a *Variety* article. I left a message from Marty. When I came back to my desk after lunch, he had returned my call. I called Vincent back, and using my best Hollywood agent voice, said, "I got a kid here like Dana Carvey, with dramatic ability." Vincent said he couldn't help me, because he only handled east coast actors, but he gave me his contact person in LA, a guy named Jackie

Johnson. I had heard of Jackie before—he was a huge comic agent. His father used to manage Merv Griffin. And now I could call him and say, "Vincent Marcel suggested that we speak." I couldn't believe how easy it was.

That night, I created a marketing campaign for myself. My plan was first and foremost to use Marty to get myself an agent and manager, and secondly, to try to get auditions for myself. I purchased an industry guide called *Comedy USA*, which listed agencies, managers, production companies, bookers—every kind of contact who could help a comedian. When I bought it, the woman who rang me up said, "What do you need it for?"

"Me," I said.

"Honey, don't you know that comedy's dead?"

I worked out the kinks in Marty's history, personality, and demeanor, creating a man would become my biggest supporter. I kept his name, because I thought Marty sounded like a menschy old guy, an irresistible grandfather type. I gave him the last name Power, because that's what I was wanted him to be—powerful. Also, I was hoping people would mistake him for a real power-agent named Marty Bauer—by the time they realized their mistake, Marty would have already won them over with his sweet demeanor and intense sales pitch.

I listened to Tony Robbins tapes. I read Dale Carnegie's *How to Make Friends and Influence People*, underlining what I considered important tips, like "Make the other person feel important, but do it sincerely!" and "Remember that a person's name is the sweetest sound in any language!" Soon, a fuller, more complete Marty Power emerged, complete with a Bronx accent and a back-story: he was retiring to Naples, Florida, and he'd promised my dying grandmother to find me new representation before he left the business for good. Why, I don't know—but it sounded good. I also learned a few Yiddish words to give Marty some flavor, and casually sprinkled them into conversation. "He's a good boy. A mensch." "Oy, the

SUCCESS JOURNAL

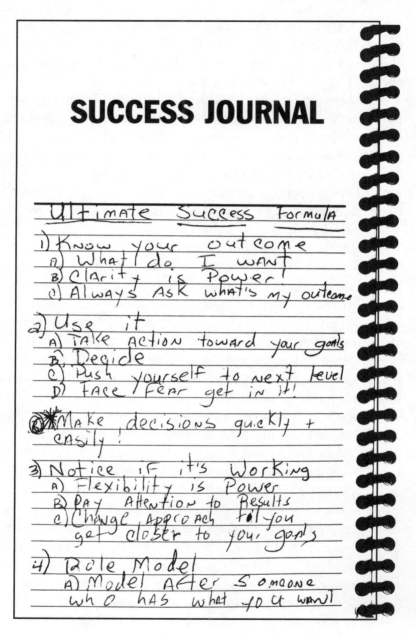

Ultimate Success Formula

1) Know your outcome
A) What do I want
B) Clarity is Power!
C) Always Ask what's my outcome

2) Use it
A) Take Action toward your goals
B) Decide
C) Push yourself to next level
D) Face Fear get in it!

⊛ Make decisions quickly + easily!

3) Notice if it's working
A) Flexibility is Power
B) Pay Attention to Results
C) Change Approach til you get closer to you goals

4) Role Model
A) Model After Someone who has what you want

"There's always a way — if you're committed."

Anthony Robbins

Welcome Frustration
when your Frustrated
you have break throughs.
It means change

Committ + Follow through.

Assignment: 2 Actions You've
been putting off, that
would immediately change
the quality in your life.

1) Work on Mon' Audition
2) Combat Roach Traps

humidity, I'm schvitzing over here." "Eh, it wasn't a bad movie. A little schmaltzy."

After Marty was born, I set up shop. I bought all the furniture I needed at St. Vincent's Church sale: an answering machine for five bucks, a clock for fifty cents, a mini-fridge for $80. The other thing I bought was a tape recorder, so I could tape all my calls. I wanted to listen to each phone call afterward, so I could practice my pitch and hone it better. I also knew there might be some funny material in there.

I named my company Power One Management, spending a crazy amount of money on letterhead stationary and envelopes. I chose gray because it seemed the most businesslike. Then, I took out a post office box. I didn't write post office box 1285 on the letterhead—I wrote Suite 1285. I assumed people would think the office was on the twelfth floor of some building on Hollywood Boulevard, near Highland Avenue, instead of its actual location, a dirty mailbox rental agency, nestled in between a donut shop and a liquor store. I got a stamp so I could imprint the envelope with Marty's name. I set up a voice mail and put a message on it, even creating an assistant for Marty named Tiffany, whose voice I impersonated as well. I bought a refrigerator magnet shaped like a mini-telephone. When pressed, it made a noise exactly like a telephone bell. I used it to make my fake office seem busy. Finally, I wrote up a whole sales pitch for myself, using all of the things that people had said about me in the past. "I, uh, got this kid. Need to get him new representation before I retire," I practiced saying to myself in the mirror. "He's a cross between Robbie Benson and James Woods. With a little Jerry Lewis sprinkled in. Just a pinch."

With the industry guide in one hand and a phone in the other, I was ready to go. I got into a routine: every morning, I woke up at nine A.M., made myself a strawberry smoothie, and called Hollywood players from my desk. "It's Marty Power calling for Bud Weinberg," I'd say.

"What's this regarding?"

"Tell Bud I have a little Jewish geography for him." They'd almost always get on the phone.

I focused mainly on the top agencies—they were too big for anyone to screw with them, so I imagined they wouldn't get suspicious about Marty. I thought that the big places were more stable and richer, and thus more apt to see the future. The little ones were usually struggling to survive, so they wouldn't be able to see outside the box. (This assumption proved true, by the way. It ended up being harder to get meetings with tiny commercial agents than with huge agencies like ICM.) I would literally stalk these people, calling at ten A.M., two P.M., and then again at five-thirty. If I got them on the phone, they would most often ask to see some tape. I'd promise to messenger some materials over that afternoon.

During lunchtime, I put together all my press kits. They included a picture, a résumé, some tape, and a handwritten note from Marty making reference to our conversation that day. Then, I'd dress up in a thrift shop-bought messenger outfit and make delivery rounds to all the agencies. I was at these places so often that the receptionists started to recognize me as the delivery guy. I always had them sign for the package, to make everything seem official.

After lunch, I'd return home and work the phones until the agencies closed. I only stayed on each call for two minutes. After that, I'd ring my fake telephone magnet to make it seem like it had multiple phones line going. I hollered at my imaginary assistant. Every once in a while, I put a piece of paper against the mouthpiece of the phone and crinkled it, so it sounded like I was on a cell phone. "Hold on," I'd say. "I'm driving through a canyon. You're breaking up." Between six-

POWER ONE MANAGEMENT
1770 North Highland Avenue, Suite #1285 * Hollywood, Ca 90028 * TEL: (213) 957-4686

4-24

Dear Pam,

I hope your feeling better, I heard your a little under the weather. Here is a tape of Jamie Kennedy from Mon. night at Igby's. I also threw in a lampoon because they put him on the cover this month. I hope you feel better.

Thanks,

thirty and seven o'clock, I'd call the agents to whom I'd dropped off tapes to follow up. I'd get back in messenger garb, deliver more packets, and return home around nine. Then, I'd then go to a club or two and do standup.

The next morning, I would start the process of calling the agents who received tapes. I generally had to call people about five times before they called me back. When they finally came to the phone, they usually said one of six things: 1) "What tape?" 2) "I haven't looked at the tape" 3) "Hmmm, is that tape on my desk?" 4) "Hey, Shannon, have you seen that tape?" 5) "Can you send the tape again?" and very rarely, the brass ring, 6) "Send him in for a meeting."

The process was exhausting, but exhilarating. Most days I'd get so engrossed in agenting that I'd forget to drink my smoothie. I remember running up the driveway to my garage every day, thinking, *I'm making it!* I was achieving real progress in my career. And I was in control.

———

After a few weeks, I started getting meetings with commercial agents. One of these meetings was with a larger company called the Sutton Agency. I sat in their upscale office, and an agent asked me how long I'd been working with Marty.

"Two years," I answered.

"You're very lucky," the well-dressed Sutton woman said. "He's a nice man."

"Do you know him?" I asked.

"No, but he's a friend of Vic's." She removed her glasses.

"Really?" I said, "Vic who owns the company?"

"Yes. The only reason you got in here is because Marty and Vic are old friends from New York. They started together in the sixties."

I couldn't believe this. Marty was building up a reputation around town! When I got home that day, there were two messages from commercial agents on my voice mail. Both wanted to sign me.

———

I couldn't get out of my contract with Fred Carver to sign with a new commercial agent, but I didn't really care. I'd done the whole commercial audition route before, unsuccessfully. It sucked. There are only so many times you can get rejected by Jack In The Box before you start to doubt yourself. I wanted to try my hand at television and film.

The first break came with a company called Morra Brezner Management. They only represented two clients, Robin Williams and Billy Crystal. At first, I was completely intimidated—I'm the guy who once lost a part to the El Pollo Loco cartoon chicken, and now I think I'm in the same league as these two? But I figured I had nothing to lose, and I sent them a tape anyway. I got a call the next day. "Marty, we saw the tapes," they said. "Betty in Buddy's office wants to meet with Jamie."

I was stunned—and excited beyond belief. I went to the meeting dressed like a seventeen-year-old kid and pitched myself exactly as they had told Marty they saw me. When I was done, I sat down on their leather couch and sipped my Evian. I didn't make eye contact because I wasn't sure if they had believed me or not. When I finally looked up, they were smiling.

Even though Morra Brezner Management didn't offer to sign me then, I started getting meetings with other television and film agents. Through their conversations with Marty, I would know what these agents thought of me and what kind of clients they were looking for. Then, I would go in and tell them exactly what they wanted to hear. When I walked into their offices, they were sitting in black leather chairs, at mahogany desks with high-tech trimmings. I knew that I was starting to move up in the world when the refreshments upgraded to water *or* juice. I always picked a water called Soleil. It sounded the best. Plus, it came in a blue bottle. This was nirvana. I mean, a few months ago I had been living in my car, and now I was entering the world of sparkling fruity beverages.

I started getting more and more interest. I had a meeting with an executive at MTV about becoming a VJ. She asked me how I'd come to work with Marty. I told her that I'd met him at a club and then he'd taken me under his wing. "He said I reminded him of Richard Pryor and he wanted to help me get started," I said. I was really starting to push it.

"Marty's great, isn't he?" she said.

"Yeah," I said.

"Now do him."

I froze.

"What do you mean?" I said.

She just looked at me and smiled. I thought, "Oh fuck! I'm about to get busted!"

"You know," she said. "Like you do in your act. On your tape, you do the impersonation of Marty."

I had totally forgotten that I'd run out of my usual tapes before I sent her a copy. I'd ended up sending her an old tape with a set that had me doing a Marty impersonation. So I said in my best Marty voice, "Look, I got a kid here . . ."

She burst into laughter and said, "God, that sounds just like him!"

"Yeah, well, I'm around him a lot," I said.

Marty called the executive that day. She was so excited about our meeting that she immediately set up another one. In the meantime, Marty's reputation kept on growing. At meeting after meeting, agents would ask me to do a Marty impression. I would do his voice, just a little bit off. They never suspected a thing.

But it wasn't all fun. Marty had a conversation with Jon Stewart's manager, who obviously didn't know that it was me on the other end of phone. He said, "That kid's way too green."

I did everything I could to keep it together, but my veneer was starting to crack. I squeaked, "Well, he's a little green, but he's good."

"Come on, Marty," he said. "He stinks. He doesn't know

```
May 9, 1994

POWER ONE MANAGEMENT
1770 North Highland Ave.
Suite #1285
Hollywood, CA 90028

Dear Power One Management:

Thank you for submitting  picture, resume and tape of JAMIE KENNEDY
for my review.

After careful consideration, I feel it is not appropriate for us to
work together at this time.

Thank you.

Warm regards,


Pamela Cole

PC/rr
encl.
```

what a set up is, he can't find his way to a punchline. He's horrible!"

It was like being sucker-punched.

"Gotta take the other line," I croaked. I hung up, took two minutes to compose myself, then went on to the next phone call.

———

I learned a lot of interesting truths about Hollywood through the process. First, almost no one will ever say no to you outright—I mean, what agent wants to be known as the guy who turned down a potential future star? Of course, no one wants to be the first to sign you either, in case you turn out to be more Dustin Diamond than Dustin Hoffman. Secondly, everyone lies. One guy who closed the door on Marty was an assistant at the William Morris agency. "He's definitely not ready yet," he told Marty.

"So, uh, when do you think the kid will be ready?" Marty asked.

"In about forty years."

Three weeks later, the same assistant s

shows. He shoved his card in my pocket, sa

excited to meet with you."

"But my manager Marty told me you said I'm not ready," I answered.

"No I didn't," he replied quickly, showing off a set of bright white chompers.

"Marty said you did."

"Nope. Didn't." He smiled. Again, the teeth. I couldn't believe him. He was flat-out lying to my face. I knew right then that he had a future in this business.

I was at a meeting with a studio executive when I had my third realization: people in the entertainment industry really didn't know what they were doing. As I was sitting in an agent's office, I looked in the corner and saw about two hundred tapes made by other hopeful comics, stacked one on top of the other. Next to them was another box labeled Kurt Cobain. It too was overflowing with tapes. I asked her what the box was for.

"That's where tapes go to die," she said. "The weird thing is that I actually have no real method for watching all these things I get sent. I just kind grab things out of the pile. Sometimes I end up putting unwatched tapes in that box when I get too backed up."

It was crazy. So much depends on sheer luck. She had just arbitrarily chosen my tape from the stack of two hundred and now I was sitting across from her. It was mind-boggling.

———

While I loved going on meetings, no one was offering to sign me. And in the meantime, I was starting to have too many close calls. Marty had developed a nice phone relationship with Amanda, a secretary at the Messina Baker Agency. Amanda ᴋed Marty to send over a tape, so I went over there at nine o'clock at night, dressed in my messenger outfit. When I walked into their lobby, I was really surprised to find that everything was open, including Rick Messina's office. I couldn't believe it. This guy had some of the most powerful clients in comedy—Drew Carey, Tim Allen—and he didn't lock his door?! I couldn't help myself; I crept into his office and started touching his belongings, hoping that some of his success would rub off on me. I touched his desk. His papers, his pens, his telephone. Next, I touched all of his pictures. And then . . . I heard a "ping."

Holy shit, I thought. *That's the elevator!* I peeked out of the office door and saw two men step out. One of them was Rick Messina.

My Hollywood life flashed before my eyes.

What the hell was he doing here? And more importantly, how the hell was I going to get out?! My first instinct was to hide under the desk. Then, I had a vision of Rick Messina, sitting in his big swively office chair, making a phone call . . . and kicking me accidentally. I couldn't believe how clichéd this whole situation was. My life had suddenly become a B movie. Probably a B movie I wanted to be in, but couldn't get an audition for. I had to get out of there.

I tip-toed out of the office very fast. Rick was coming in from the left. I was going to the right. I waited behind a wall and ducked into the elevator. Then I realized that I still had the tape in my hand. I snuck back in, darting behind various plants and file cabinets, and dropped the tape on Amanda's desk. In the background, Rick cleared his throat. I dropped down to my hands and knees and crawled toward an exit sign. I made my way through the door, quietly opened it, and walked out. Then I tore down six flights of stairs. When I got to the street, I ran down the block. The next day, Amanda from Messina Baker called Marty. They wanted to set up a meeting.

Marty was generating heat. It was time for the next step, so I decided to put together a showcase. A showcase is when eight or ten comedians get together, invite a bunch of industry people to come out, and each perform their tightest six minutes. The showcase I put together was at Igby's, which was a pretty big club at the time. The owner said that if we got enough people to the club, he would waive his fee and we could put on the show for free—we might even make a little money out of it. I was hoping that when the industry people saw the act and heard the audience, who would all be my friends, they would say, "I've got to be in business with this guy."

I practiced my standup routine every night, completely terrified. What if I bombed and all of this work had been for nothing? The evening of the comedy showcase finally arrived. I packed the place with everyone I'd ever met in LA and gave myself the prime spot—fourth. The comedian before me had a great set, which only made me more petrified. Then, my turn. I walked out onto the stage and looked into the audience. All of my agent contacts were there. This was it—the do or die moment.

The first joke I did was called "Hot Cousin." I started out, "I have a really beautiful cousin. Sometimes I see her at family get-togethers and think to myself . . . *how* retarded would our kids be?"

BOOM! The place exploded with laughter. And suddenly, I had no fear. I went on like I didn't have a care in the world—and the audience loved it. When I finished my act, the applause was some of the loudest I'd ever received.

Afterward, I went outside to get some fresh air. I was sweaty and nervous. Suddenly, I heard someone call my name. I turned around. There were all these people with business cards in my face. ICM, APA, Shapiro West, Brillstein-Grey. Everyone was talking at once. The night had been a success.

The next day, Marty made follow-up calls to everyone. ICM wanted a meeting. So did Brillstein-Grey. Then, the Agency for the Performing Arts (APA) called, requesting the unthinkable.

"We want you to come in with Jamie and meet the whole agency," they told Marty.

Marty nearly choked on his toast. "Uh, I'll be in Florida all week, finalizing the condo timeshare biz," I rasped.

"What about next week?" they replied.

I needed an excuse. Lunch with Bobcat Goldthwait? No, he wasn't hot enough. Milton Berle? Wait, was Milton Berle even alive? Fuck it. "I've got a, uh . . . funeral?"

"What about the week after?"

"Can't. I got Rodney Dangerfield's grandkid's bar mitzvah."

Finally, they agreed to see me alone. They sounded a little hurt, though.

I went to the meeting, where they made me an offer of representation. It was ridiculously satisfying. At the end, just for fun, I said, "Marty wanted to apologize for not being here."

They walked me down to the garage and I drove off. Even though I was still in my shitty car, I felt invincible. I owned my own destiny. I had been waiting for this moment my whole life. Marty's career was over . . . and after five years, mine was finally beginning.

11.

Peaches and
(Bailey's Irish) Cream

The world is round and the place which may
seem like the end may also be
only the beginning.
—Ivy Baker Priest

Why I Haight Ashbury

After my comedy showcase, I went on a lot of meetings, but I didn't sign anywhere. I felt like every place was too big for me, and I was scared of getting lost in the shuffle. I needed someone who could give me personal attention. Then, a manager named Peach Schnapps started trying to sign me. Peach was eccentric. She wore a fur coat in the summer, drove a Lotus station wagon, and drank wine out of the box. She came on really strong, calling me every day and giving me the hard sell.

"Have you signed with anyone yet?" she'd say.

I'd say, "I'm still weighing my options."

"Well Jamie, if it's not gonna be you, I'll just get someone else," she'd say.

It was a total mind game . . . and it worked. I signed on. Two months later, Peach got me my first big gig—a spot in the San Francisco comedy competition. This was a major coup. The San Francisco comedy competition had been around for twenty years, predating the Aspen and Montreal Comedy Festivals. It was a very prestigious event in the comedy community. In 1976, the first year of the Comedy Competition, Robin Williams came in second. Dana Carvey won in 1977. Ellen Degeneres was first runner-up in 1985. Peach was able to get me one of the forty competition spots because she was friends with the organizers. She said, "Your act needs work, but you have a lot of potential. If they see what I see, you'll start building a name for yourself."

The competition itself ran for three weeks and was divided into four rounds—two concurrent sets of preliminaries, a semi-final round, and the final competition. In the first preliminary round, we were divided into two groups of twenty. For the next six nights, all twenty of us would do seven-minute acts at a different club. For the six nights after that, the second group of twenty would do the same. Then, the top guys from each group would go head to head against each other and so on.

I started out in the first group of comedians. I was confident that I would make it to the top ten and hopeful that I would get to the top five. Well . . . that didn't quite happen. Instead, I bombed—*every single night*. (Theme!)

I'd never performed for paying customers over a consistent period of time. I had just done open mics in front of audiences made up of other comedians. As it turned out, real people didn't get me at all. The competition was a traditional joke-teller fest where you had to hit them every two seconds—

punch, punch, punch. All I had were weird characters in vaguely-thought-out sketches. I wasn't connecting.

The whole experience was not very pleasurable. I didn't have a car, so I had to bum rides from other comics to get to clubs. I couldn't even afford a hotel. I stayed at the Chinatown YMCA one night and slept on the floor of some club another night. Midway through the week, I became friends with a comic named Cash who let me stay at his parents' house. There was nothing to do during the days but walk around and get condescending stares from people in coffee shops.

———

After our final night, the results came in. I placed thirty-eighth out of forty. The only people below me were a guy who only spoke French and a girl who never showed up. Everything was in the toilet. Right when I was about to find a bus back to LA, Peach called. "Buy a ticket to New York," she said. "You're going to audition for *Saturday Night Live*." No way!

I'd actually been waiting to hear about New York for a while. A few weeks back, Peach had arranged for me to meet Lorne Michaels in LA. I was so excited—it was my dream coming true before my eyes. She said, "They're really only looking for a new girl. But I told him that he had to see you."

"That's cool," I said.

"And you might have to wait a few minutes when you go in to meet with him."

I went to Lorne's office at two o'clock.

At seven, he poked his head out and said, "I hear you do a lot of characters and impressions."

"Yes, sir."

"Would you like to come to New York and audition for me?"

"Yeah, sure!"

OFFICIAL STANDINGS

1	Justin	Stern	55.96
2	Ray	Korn	55.21
3	Tommy	Porgin	54.56
4	Adam	Scott	53.73
5	Vinnie	"High Voltage" Terrino	52.16
6	Don	Zogafagus	50.89
7	William	Handle	50.76
8	Gary	Thompson	49.59
9	Phillip	Langfeld	49.51
10	Charlie	Renally	49.35
11	Mark	Ureaka	49.03
12	Pat	Bardulli	48.69
13	Jason	Matthews	48.40
14	Les	Jenkins	48.17
15	Rich	Short	47.88
16	Harold	Middleton	47.67
17	Sean	Stevens	47.33
18	Teddy	Gentry	47.31
19	Tony	Nelson	47.04
20	Josh	Giraldi	46.72
21	Charlie	Lee	46.27
22	Eliza	Rupp	45.12
23	Randy	Strathan	45.01
24	Nick	Rolletter	44.60
25	Grant	Wachkowski	44.14
26	Cash	Levy	43.79
27	Barry	Nash	43.51
28	Al	Rueben	43.13
29	George	Labaue	43.01
30	Janice	Kazlyn	42.66
31	Doug	Delvechio	42.28
32	Riff	Kettleworth	41.73
33	Blair	Kelly	39.64
34	Steve	Karackas	39.18
35	BJ	Carter	38.24
36	Morris	Campbell	37.11
37	Yassir	Smith	36.23
38	Jamie	Kennedy	35.51
39	Roland	Rousseau	35.37
40	Alice	Lasky	31.74

"Okay, see you there," he said. Then he left and went to dinner.

————

After receiving Peach's phone call, I took the next plane out of San Francisco. Even though I'd grown up an hour and a half away from New York, this was only my second time there—and the first time was when I was eight years old, for three hours. I didn't even know what New York was. I was from suburban Pennsylvania—I knew what drinking in a field or grabbing a tit in someone's basement was.

I had my eight-minute audition for Lorne at a club called Standup New York. I auditioned with Molly Shannon, who did her Mary Katherine Gallagher Catholic schoolgirl character. She didn't get on the show that night, but six months later she reauditioned and was cast. My set went pretty well. I was hopeful. The next day I called Peach from the train station. "Did you hear anything?"

"Do you have your tickets? Do you have your bags?" she asked.

"Yeah, I have everything," I said. "So?"

"Did you check in?" she asked, totally avoiding the conversation.

"Yeah. So . . . ?"

She paused. "You didn't get it."

"Why?" I asked.

"You didn't do enough political impressions," Peach said.

"You didn't tell me I had to do political impressions."

"Don't be silly. Of course I did."

"No you didn't," I said. "If I had known that, I would have worked on my Zöe Baird."

"Oh well, what can you do?" she said. "That's the way the cork pops."

<u>Journal Entries</u>

Aug 8, 1994

2 A.M. I feel good. I'm on a Greyhound, on my way to Frisco. I'm excited, anxious, nervous. I really love life right now. 12 p.m. The ride's cool. I've been on the bus for eleven hrs. All I keep thinking about is my thinning hair. What happens if I go bald? Do I only get bald guy roles. I fucking hate it. I wish I could just have my hair.

Aug 9, 1994

Just got a room at the chinatown YMCA. I'm paying my dues but I love it. I get to work out and use the pool. I'm looking forward to tonight. I'm gonna take so many chances during this contest!

Aug 10, 1994

I feel good. I placed last, last night but that's okay, because at least I'm not middle of the road.

Aug 11, 1994

I didn't make it to the top five tonight,
but fuck that. I should have beat at least
one or two of those guys. It dosen't
matter though. They all know what I can do.
It feels like a relief to have no expectations.
Hey, I'm ready. I do what I do. They either
like me or they don't. Bottom line is I'm
psyched.

Aug 12, 1994

If I were up here long enough, I would be
questioning how funny I am.

Aug 13, 1994

I'm like a fucking Martian. I walk around
the malls and sit in the park all day. At
night, I do five minutes of material for
people who hate me. I'm counting the
minutes. I'm counting the seconds. I'm going
fucking berseek. I don't know who I am
anymore.

Aug 14, 1994

I can't stand it here anymore. I'm so
depressed. It's so hard going up in these
rooms and not getting RESPECT!

Aug 15, 1994

I fucking hate San Francisco. I hate
these fuckin grunge rocker hippie types.
They've got blue hair, a goatee, an earing
in they're nose and a Ralph Lauren
chain wallet with 5 credit cards and
fresh hundred dollar bills all alphabetized
in a money clip. Pick a side man. What
are you rebelling against? Bloomingdale's?
Everybody up here tries to be so smart
and deep. You know what's deep? My Asshole.
Why don't you climb in there and snuff
around?

Aug 16, 1994

I'm at the San Francisco airport on my way
to New York. I'm going to audition for SNL!
I can't wait!

Aug 17, 1994

Tonight's my SNL Audition! ~~SAN FRAN CAN~~
lick my SAC!! Eat a dick, I'm
gonna be on SNL. I don't need you,
I don't need nobody!!!

Set List For <u>Tonite</u>

1) Alan Rickman as Forrest Gump.
2) Transvestite President
3) Karate Accountant
4) Ham lady
5) Morrison Kindergarten Teacher
6) Gay Jack Nicholson

Aug 18, 1994

Well everybody's speculation was wrong, including my own! The fact that I'd be perfect for SNL - I wasn't. But even though I placed near last in San Fran AND SNL said no, I feel really great! I know I'm good. I know it. Charles Manson Auditioned for the Monkees and didn't make it, And now look at his career. No, I really feel good. Okay, maybe I'm somewhat bummed. But maybe this just isn't my shot. I mean, look at Jim Carrey. He does every impression in the book and I heard SNL passed on him, twice. That's why I'm not bummed. I just have to rebuild. I know I've got something. I know I'm not nuts. I know it! This buisness is About proving yourself. You have to prove yourself over AND over again. I just haven't proven myself enough yet. I'm young AND I'm handsome. No worries. Fuck SNL. Fuck 'em. Fuck. Fuck. Fuck Fuck fuck fuck fuck fuck fuck fuck fuck. Fuck. Fuck. Fuck.

I was so frustrated. The main reason I was even *doing* standup was to get enough characters together to audition for *Saturday Night Live*. Now I was back to square one.

An Elf with a Future

After I got back from New York, I caught a break. MTV wanted to cast me in a test pilot called *On the Loose*. The show was going to feature me breaking into different high-end events, and seeing if I could attain some goal while I was there. The pilot was shot at a tennis tournament in Westwood. I had to find Brooke Shields, who was dating Andre Agassi, and get her to sign a copy of a *Blue Lagoon* poster. During the two-day shoot, I was under so much pressure to find Brooke that I lost my mind—and my poster along with it. I snuck into the postgame conference on the last night and talked Andre Agassi into having Brooke sign a racket instead. He actually did it, which was really cool, considering that I'd been chasing his poor ass for the past two days.

Then, MTV decided not to pick up the show. I started thinking. At this point, I'd been rejected by *In Living Color*. I'd been rejected by *SNL*. And now, my pilot was dead. The comedy angle wasn't working for me. It was time to focus on just being an actor.

Peach was trying to get me work, but it's hard to break in a new actor, and she just wasn't hungry enough. Meanwhile, I was starving—literally. So I decided to reincarnate Marty to work alongside her. I asked MTV for a copy of the pilot so I could update my reel. They said, "Sorry, we don't give out pilots."

What bullshit. Without that tape, people wouldn't cast me in other things. So I broke into MTV's offices in the middle of the night, dressed as a delivery guy. I stole the tape, made copies, and put it back in their library without anyone noticing. It was bad enough that I had to lie to get an agent, now I had to be MacGyver.

Marty got me a few auditions by sending my tapes out to casting directors and producers. One of my first was for a show called *California Dreams*, the sister show of *Saved By The Bell*. After I had finished reading for the part of "Sea Kelp," the casting director, Robin Lippin, said, "That was good, Jamie. Thank you." She was very nice about it, but this was standard blow-off procedure.

As I walked out of the audition, I thought about how much I wanted this part, how ready I felt to start working. Over the past few months, I had been gaining some traction on the open mic circuit. A writer for the Redondo Beach News had seen me perform and written a cover story about me called "An Elf with a Future." Granted, it was only a local beach paper, but it was still the cover. The story had just come out, and I had the paper in my bag. Just as I was about to leave the building, I happened to notice it—and it made me feel like I had to take action.

All of my acting teachers had told me over and over that I should never talk to a casting director after an audition. I was just supposed to do the scene and leave—be respectful. Approaching someone afterwards gave off a desperate vibe. But the thing is, I *was* desperate. And I just didn't care what anyone said anymore.

I just stopped in my tracks and thought, *I really need this job and I'm going to fight for it.* I knew I could be Sea Kelp! I knew I could deliver the line, "Let's party."

I marched back into Robin's office and approached her desk. I said, "I know that you're seeing a lot of people for this part. But I want to let you know that I could do it in my sleep. And I really need a job. And just to let you know, there's this guy in Redondo Beach who believes in me too." I took the magazine out of my bag. It was my last copy. I handed it over to her and said, "You can keep it." She took the paper and told me she would read it.

Then, I went home and obsessed about the conversation for hours. Why had I done that? Had I come off desperate? Did I just screw myself? Fuck. Two hours later, I got a call. It was Robin. She was actually calling for Marty, but I accidentally picked up the phone.

"This is Jamie," I said.

"Heyyyy Jamie," Robin said, sounding a little scared of me. "Isn't this Marty's phone line?"

"Yeah, he's in the can," I said. Now she probably thought I was even more of a psycho.

"I'll just ask you then," she said. "Can you start tomorrow at ten?"

"Really?" I said.

"You bet."

I hung up the phone and literally did a jig. It was such a turning point for me, in terms of my life, career and mindset. Like, just ask and ye shall receive. It totally could have backfired—she could have thought I was a psycho-aggressive and pushy actor (which I was). But I appealed to her and she was compassionate. She took a shot. Maybe she believed in me. Or maybe knew that she wasn't casting *Macbeth* and just said, "What the hell?"

California Dreams ended up opening doors for me. I did the show once and they liked me, so they called me back again. So now I had a tiny little cushion of money.

Mad Love

I was doing standup comedy one night when I noticed a cute female comedienne named Monica waiting for her turn to go on stage. Now, I knew I wasn't supposed to touch a girl who touches a microphone, but I couldn't help myself. I had an infatuation with crazy chicks. I still do. Like, I love girls who throw things at you. The whole thing is very animalistic. I end up thinking, *Wow, what passion. I wonder how mad she gets in bed?* So even though I knew better, I couldn't help myself from asking her out.

The whole time Monica and I were dating, I felt like I was in the movie *Mad Love*. She was so funny—but so nuts. She was in, like, ten different twelve-step addiction groups. I think she might have been addicted to them.

Our first sexual experience was a total nightmare. As soon as she put my penis inside of her, I came. I screamed, "Get off, get off, I came!"

"You fucking idiot. Don't you have any self control?" she said.

"I never get laid," I said.

She ran to the bathroom and started cupping her hand under the faucet, filling it with water. Then, she started throwing the water inside herself, up her vaginal canal. I screamed, "What are you doing? You're giving the sperm more of a river to swim in. You're just aiding their cause."

I couldn't be a father now! I had to stop them! I decided to try to dry her up. I ran to the kitchen, rifled through the cabinets, grabbed a bag of flour, ran back into the bathroom, and then started throwing flour at her vagina. It was like I was making pussy cookies. She screamed, "Stop! Stop!" I just kept throwing flour on her until she was white as a ghost. She didn't get pregnant, but I think she got a yeast infection.

————

For the first time in the five years that I'd been in LA, I actually felt like I was in a pretty good place, professionally. I'd gotten my SAG card, an agent, a manager, a commercial, a guest spot on a TV show, and a crazy girlfriend. Then, PAAAAAIIIII-INNNNN.

12.

The Kidney Stays in the Picture

Attention to health is life's greatest hindrance.
—Plato

Zee Size of a Zoftball

From the time that I was seventeen, I got these dull numbing pains in my back about once a year. They felt like someone was applying constant pressure to my lower back. Then, when I was twenty-four, the pains grew worse and more frequent, and within the year, I had them every day.

I started going to doctors, but no one could figure out what was wrong with me. At first they thought it was skeletal pain—something wrong with my bones. Then, they decided it was muscular. They did more tests—nothing. The pain got worse. Finally, I was referred to a urologist—this German doctor at UCLA. He looked at an x-ray and announced, "Your kidney iz zee size of a zoftball. Ve are going to go in there and drain zee kidney."

"How do you do that?" I asked.

"Ve put a stent in you," he said.

Basically, a stent is a plastic tube that the doctors jam through your penis, which slowly drains your kidney of all the toxins it should be releasing on its own. I don't recommend it. I had the thing in for six months. It killed when I got a boner and my urine smelled like day-old tuna.

After all the fluid was out, my drained kidney was the size of the pea. The urologist said, "It iz medically recommended to remove a kidney that iz functioning at less than tventy percent."

"What's my kidney functioning at?" I asked.

"Three."

"WHAT?!??"

"I am going to have to remove zee kidney."

I was floored. In the span of a month, I'd gone from having some back pain to needing surgery that would remove an organ—a major one. It was devastating. I was scared of dying, not to mention pissed off at the basic injustice of it all. I mean, why me? I didn't smoke or drink or eat read meat. I already had a pacemaker. How much did I have to pay the Gods of Health?

It was just so depressing. I was at this phase in my life where I was finally starting to get somewhere. Every time I would come home, I'd tear up the driveway because I was so excited to start making phone calls again. Things were moving. When I heard the kidney news, it really set me back psychologically. I remember slumping up the driveway, thinking about how everything was so pointless. Nothing I was doing mattered. I was losing my hair, I didn't get *Saturday Night Live*, I didn't get my MTV pilot, my boners hurt, and now I was losing a kidney. And I was scared out of my mind. Was I going to have to spend the rest of my life on dialysis? Was I going to die?

I went into total denial. I called up my doctor and told him that I wasn't going to have the operation. There was a long pause before he said, "Vell, you have to."

"Vell, I don't want to," I answered back.

"Vell, then you have, you know, problem."

"What if I just keep the tube in there?" I asked, trying to bargain.

"You can't keep a tube in your kidney forever. The kidney vill blow back up again. Eet could get infected. And then, you could die vithin forty-eight hours," he said.

"I'll call you later," I said.

I embarked on a mission to save my kidney, going to other doctors and acupuncturists and Chinese herbalists. Everyone told me the same thing—I had a bad organ in my body. I was at a loss. I called my doctor again and asked if there were some medicines I could take. "Vat," he asked, "to fix a dead kidney? Let me know, I vant to sell them."

"Look," he continued. "You can live your life vith one kidney. Zee other kidney is vorking fine. Ve'll take it out and you'll be back in no time. Lots of people do it."

"I don't have time to lose a kidney," I said. "I have a *Ned and Stacey* audition in the morning!" My priorities were a little out of order.

Eventually, I realized that I couldn't let my health problems deter me. I told myself that I would just have the surgery, recuperate and get back to normal as soon as possible. But there was another problem. I didn't have medical insurance or money to pay for the operation. "Okay," said my doctor, "here is vat ve're going to do," he said. "I vill vaive my fee and ve vill do it at a county hospital. Everything vill be free because it vill be paid for by zee state. I'll come dovn to the county hospital to do zee operation and afterward their doctors vill look after you." Just like that. He said it so nonchalantly, like it was no big deal. It was a $21,000 operation and he waived his whole fee. It was the greatest display of generosity I'd ever seen.

In order to get the surgery for free, I had to go to Torrance hospital, which isn't exactly a place that instills confidence in the health profession. It was the kind of place that had malicious nurses and blood on the floors from the day before. You went under and there was a fifty/fifty chance you were coming back. It was pretty close to the ghettos in South Central, so it was littered with gang-bangers and gunshot victims. My father, who, along with my mother, had flown in for the surgery, felt that it was his duty to make conversation with all of them. One guy had been shot in the neck. My dad said to him, "Hey, buddy. What happened to you?"

"Drive-by shooting," he whispered.

"Somebody drove a car and shot you?" my dad asked. "Why, that's a sin."

The guy just stared at him.

The procedure to remove my kidney was called a laparoscopy. I was actually one of the first people to have this type of operation on a kidney. Basically, what they do is make a small incision in your back, insert a miniature camera so the doctor can monitor your internal organs, vacuum out the kidney, and close everything up.

Right before I went into surgery, my evil nurse gave me a shot of Demerol. I yelped in pain. She said, "If you think it hurts now, just wait till they suck that whole kidney out 'choo."

The operation went well. In fact, it was such a success that my case is now often used as a model during medical conferences. I didn't know that then. All I knew was that I was in an excruciating amount of pain. I mean PAIN!!!! I couldn't move. If I breathed in or out, it hurt. I was too sedated to talk. It was like my chest had an anvil on it. I was hooked up to what seemed like twenty IVs and had tubes up my nose and down my throat. I felt like Linda Lovelace. I couldn't eat, I couldn't drink, and I couldn't go to the bathroom. This was as bad as life could get. Except it wasn't.

If I Didn't Have This Bag, I'd Fuck You Up

My girlfriend Monica came to visit me after my surgery. She brought a book of Henny Youngman's jokes with her, and read them to me, trying to cheer me up. They were all kind of purposely stupid, like, "When Moses sat on the top of Mount Sinai, you know what he said? This would be a good place for a hospital!" It was all I could do to stay awake.

"Laugh, laugh!" she urged me. I just couldn't do it. I was in too much pain to even blink.

Then, out of nowhere, we heard this tiny little laugh, like, "Heh heh heh." It came from behind the curtain separating me from my roommate. I couldn't see him and he couldn't see me. Monica ignored him and kept telling jokes. Then the voice said, "Yeah, that's a really funny one."

"Who is that?" she asked. "Who are you?"

The voice just kept laughing and coughing. Then, silence. "Do you think he's okay?" she asked me. "Sir?" There was no response. She whispered, "That guy's really weird." Monica started rubbing my arm. "I think you should try to sit up," she said. "You can't stay in bed forever. I mean, you've been out of surgery for two hours already."

Then, the voice again. "My name's Myke," it said. "M-Y-K-E, no I."

Monica didn't know what to do. "Oh, Myke like dyke," she said.

"What are you in here for?" asked Myke, no I.

"I'm here visiting my boyfriend," Monica said. "He's here because he had his kidney removed. Why are you here?"

There was a long pause.

"Got stabbed with a pool cue," he said. "The fat end."

I started to get worried.

"Ripped my insides to shreds, punctured my small intestine," Myke continued. "Now I gotta wear this shit sack. That fuck is dead. Found out where he lives."

"Wow, that's horrible," Monica said. "But you shouldn't be fighting."

I was thinking, *Holy shit, she's challenging the guy with the shit sack?*

"He cheap-shotted me," Myke protested.

"Well, that's karma," she shot back. "What goes around, comes around."

I began to breathe quicker, into my tube.

"It's true," she said, looking at me, righteously.

"I didn't start nothin'," Myke said.

"Whatever," she said.

"You don't believe me, you stupid piece of fish?" Mike screamed.

"Excuse me? What did you call me, you filthy little shit?" she screamed right back. Then, she turned to me. "Are you going to let him speak to me like that?!"

I could barely breathe, let alone move, I was in so much pain. All I could do was just look at Monica with a petrified expression.

"You had your kidney removed, not your balls!" she shouted and stormed out of the room.

Myke was silent for a minute. Then he started to speak again, "Are you fucking with me, Jamie? Cause you don't want to fuck with me! If I wasn't wearing this bag, man. You're lucky I can't see your face. I don't forget faces."

How did he know my name? He'd been listening to our whole conversation. I practically gagged on my breathing tube.

"If I didn't have this fuckin' bag," he continued, "I'd fuck you up!"

A few hours later, I felt good enough to watch TV. I turned the set onto a channel that was playing cartoons. Suddenly, the channel changed to *Taxi Driver*. I changed it back to cartoons. Back to *Taxi Driver*. Back to cartoons. Out of nowhere, a bedpan went flying at the TV from Myke's side of the room. "Leave it!" he screamed.

The next day, things got more disturbing. I was lying there lifeless, a tube down my throat, watching TV. Then, I dropped my remote on the floor. I reached down to pick it up, but I couldn't get to it. Then, I heard a noise, like, "Ohhhhhhhh," and some slurping sounds. From behind the curtain, Myke said, "Hmmmm, you really can hum, sugar." I couldn't believe it—Myke had a girl back there? I tried to reposition myself, so I could see what was going on. As I shifted around, I knocked four bottles of pills off of my nightstand. They all fell on the ground with a resounding crash. All the moaning and slurping stopped. Silence. I sat there, tube in my throat, terrified and frozen in position.

"Fucking perv," Myke said. The slurping began again.

Then, my parents came to visit. My mom handed me a can of kidney beans. "Your sister bought you these," my mom said. "Isn't she funny?"

I couldn't even summon the strength to nod. My dad lit up a cigarette. My mom kept talking, "We went to dinner last night at the Pantry. Have you ever been there? Oh my lands, we got a prime rib, green beans, and a baked potato for $5.99. Plus a large bowl of rice pudding for desert."

From behind the curtain, Myke piped in, "You should see what they got on Sunday."

"Oh!" my mom said. "You have a neighbor." I wanted to warn her that he was psychotic, but I couldn't speak.

Myke continued, "They got the tallest short stack of pancakes you ever seen. OJ, hash browns, bacon, and two eggs. Plus free refills."

My mother's eyes lit up. She'd found a partner in frugality. "Is someone smoking?" Myke asked.

My father grumbled, "Yeah." He went to put it out.

"Could I bum one off ya?" Myke said.

"Well sure, buddy," my dad said, perking up.

This was awful. For the next few hours, I drifted in and out of consciousness while Myke won my parents' sympathy by telling them all about his shit sack. "I tell ya, Bob. I'm a regular at the place. I know the guy Tommy who works behind the bar. I've had a few beers, just standing there, talking to Rita, about to break a nice rack. I hear someone yell out, 'Myke.' I turn around. Next thing I know—I've got a nineteen ounce Brunswick in my gut. I'm surprised it went in."

"Oh my god," my dad said.

"That's just awful," my mom said.

"Yeah. I was skeeeeeeeeewered," Myke said. "That's why I'm wearing this taco shell. You'd think they'd give me something to knock me out."

My mother looked ready to cry. "Here," she said, handing him my Percodan. "Jamie doesn't even touch his."

I wanted to scream, "Mom, no!" But I still couldn't speak.

The next day, Myke ran out of painkillers. He started freaking out, screaming and demanding more. Our evil nurse came in, laughed and said, "Y'all got some habit. Too bad I ain't yo pusher!"

"Please?" said Myke.

"I got some St. Joseph's chewables," she said, laughing. She handed him some Tylenol and left.

Myke shouted, "My asshole's on my hip and all you can give me is fuckin' Tylenol?! You fucking cunt!" He started in on me, "Hey Jamie. I know things aren't the best between us. But can I have one of your pills, man? Come on! Give me one of your pills!"

I just sat there, motionless.

He screamed, "GIVE ME THE PILLS, YOU FUCK!" Then, he threw his bedpan at the wall. A ripping noise. Mike screamed in pain. "Owwwww! My shit bag broke! Nurse! My fucking bag popped!"

I glanced down at the floor. It looked like a colostomy pizza.

The next day, I got my voice back. When my parents came in, I warned them to stay away from Myke.

"Why?" my dad asked.

"He's been threatening me," I said.

"Myke? You're hallucinating. He's a good guy."

It was too late. He had already entrenched himself in their hearts.

On day four, our nurse came in. She said, "The doctor said you're pissin' clear."

"What does that mean?" asked my mom.

"He got to leave today, Miss Thang."

"But it's only been four days!" my mom said.

"Don't let his cryin' wolf fool you. Shit, I've seen amputees heal faster," she said.

"What about me?" asked Myke from behind his curtain.

"Yo ass is going to C Ward. Wit the cripples."

"I ain't no fucking cripple!"

"The hell you ain't!"

I got my stuff together and the nurse wheeled me out of the room. From behind the curtain Myke spoke, in a very meek voice: "Hey Jamie, you should give me your number so we can hang out sometime."

I didn't respond.

"Oh, you're too good for me? Okay," he said, in a menacing voice. "But just remember. I've seen your face, Jamie! And I don't forget faces."

I thought, *Has he seen my face?* I didn't know. I'd never seen his. He began to laugh eerily as the nurse wheeled me away. I haven't had a roommate since.

Lucky

I left the hospital, all banged up and bruised. After about a week of sitting in my apartment, I got stir crazy and decided to walk to 7-11. I had to move slowly, because my stitches hadn't come out, but I was enjoying the walk—it was a nice, warm night. Then, out of nowhere, a guy jumped out at me from some bushes. "Hey holmes," he said. As soon as the words were out of his mouth, I knew that I had walked into something really uncomfortable.

"Hey, what's up?" I said and turned to walk across the street. Before the words were even out of my mouth, I felt another guy come up from behind me and put a rather large knife up against my back—right next to my good kidney. It felt porno big.

"Stay cool," he said. "I got a gun in my pocket."

The first guy said, "Holmes, I want your wallet." He spoke very calmly, like he was giving directions.

"Sure, sure," I said, attempting to placate him. I tried to put one hand over my kidney and reach for my wallet with the other. Then it dawned on me. I didn't have any money.

I didn't know how to act, so I pleaded with him gently, "I don't have any money. Here, take my shoes and watch instead."

He tightened his grip around my neck. "You know what?" he said. "We've been robbing people all night and no one's got any fucking money. You know how that makes me feel?"

"Please," I said.

"I wanna stick you just for that, ese."

Great, because everyone else was broke, I had to pay. I started to pray. Then I started to think about all the different mugging scenarios that could play out, wondering, *Is he going to shoot me or stab me? If he stabs me that's really gonna hurt. And if it goes through the kidney, then I'll have to be on dialysis and I'll need a transplant. That would suck. If he shoots me, how long would I have until I bled to death? Or maybe he'd just shoot me in the calf. But then I'd have a limp.*

He nudged me and I started taking off my shoes and my watch. "I'm not worth it," I begged. "You don't want to waste your time killing me." Then, I remembered seeing a show on the Discovery Channel that said you should humanize yourself to the attacker. "And I have a baby," I pleaded. "He's a new-born. Donald."

I gave him my pants. He looked at my stuff and said, "Okay holmes, I'm gonna let go and count to ten. After ten I'm gonna start shooting your ass. So you better run." He let go and I started sprinting away in my underwear, never turning around once. I heard him following behind me, step for step. I zig-zagged between the cars, hoping that if he did start shooting, I would avoid any bullets. I ran all the way to the top of a street, where I saw a cop. I told him what happened. He looked at me in my underwear and said, "You're lucky."

In the end, losing the kidney made me realize that our time here was limited. At the same time, it made me even more fanatical and obsessive—it made me want to run faster. Even now, when I feel great, I think about how we're just brittle, flesh and bones. We can get torn down any moment.

Recap of 1994

1) Got Vans Commercial
2) Got SAG Card
3) Got Agent
4) Got Manager
5) Got California Dreams (twice!)
6) Got Mugged
7) Got Kidney removed

13.

Still Jamie from the Blockbuster

A discovery is said to be an accident
meeting a prepared mind.
—Albert von Szent-Gyorgyi

Numbers Game

Monica and I were lying in her bed one Sunday morning, when she said, "Show me your reel." That meant she wanted to see what I had done acting-wise—showcasing your compilation reel was a common ritual among LA actor couples. It was also common to have it on you 24/7. I put my tape in the VCR. She watched it, started giggling and kissing me, then said, "You're great. Why don't you do more commercials?"

I said, "Because my agent sucks."

She said, "I'm taking you into my agency tomorrow. You should be working." Monica was bossy like that, but I liked it.

The next day, Monica marched me into her agent's office. She told her agent, "You should sign him." Her agent looked at my tape and said, "I like it. Why doesn't he work?"

Monica said, "Because his agent sucks."

Her agent said, "Let's show the boss."

The boss, Julie, looked at it and said, "I like it. Why doesn't he work?"

"Because his agent sucks," they both replied.

"I hate sucky agents," Julie said. She turned to me, "This is all a numbers game, honey. You're not being submitted properly. You need to go out on stuff where you can improvise and show off your personality." Then she signed me on the spot. It was amazing. Here I'd spent a year and a half trying to be celibate, thinking it would *help* my career. If I had known that sleeping around would get me an agent, I would have gone there a lot sooner.

The first audition Julie got me was at five o'clock that same afternoon. I didn't get a callback. My next audition was two days later, for a Blockbuster Video commercial. Their direction was, "Be natural! Spontaneous! Have fun with it!" Whatever that meant. Then, they asked, "If Robin Williams went into a Blockbuster, what would he do?"

I just went off. I made up characters, did an impression of Tommy Lee Jones as the Lion King, and did a character called Daniel Day Jerry Lewis, which was Jerry Lewis doing scenes from *In the Name of the Father*. They called the next day and hired me. I didn't even have to go on a callback. It was the biggest thing I had ever gotten in my whole career and it happened in a week.

I was one of four people who were hired to be part of this new promotion, the Blockbuster Entertainment Team. First, we shot a series of commercials and print ads in the United States. Then, they flew us to Europe to be Blockbuster representatives.

We traveled through Ireland, England, France, and Prague, bringing good cheer to various Blockbusters. It was crazy—our posters were all over all the stores. Plus, there was an air of mystery about us: we could show up anywhere, anytime. We were like the Jareds of European Blockbuster. We even had our own theme song.

The weird thing is that I had applied for a job at the Blockbuster on Sunset in the early 90s, which I didn't get. They said I wasn't qualified. Even weirder—I won a Blockbuster Best Supporting Actor award for my part in *Scream II*, just a few years later. My category was slated to be announced after Julia Roberts's and I was a little nervous about following her. Then, they cut my category because of time constraints. They mailed me my award instead. It had a chip in it.

————

About nine months after we started dating, Monica and I broke up. I loved her, but we fought non-stop. After that, I didn't have any time for a girlfriend. I did have time for booty calls, though, random girls I could call when I wanted to rub up against something warm and soft. The poorer I looked, the easier it was to meet them. Ever since I grew my hair long, girls felt like they had to take care of me. They would bring me dinner because they thought I couldn't operate the stove. Then, they'd touch my hair and say, "You look lost. Should I suck your dick?" Empty? Sure it was. Efficient? You bet your ass.

Monday Morning Quarterback

Before I got my Blockbuster job, I had absolutely no money. Within one day, I made a lot. But even though I had a nice little cushion now, I was still so paranoid. All I could think about was how I could lose it in a heartbeat. I was determined to save as much as I could.

I rented an apartment that was a box, a total dump. Its one window had bars. I never even had to have a credit check when I moved in. The woman who showed me the place was wifty. She just said, "Okay, you like? Here you go."

"Where do I send my checks?" I asked.

"Oh, you know. We'll get them." she said. Then, she handed me the key and walked out.

Eventually, I found my landlord's address and mailed in the rent. The landlord never cashed my checks, though. He was a hundred years old and too busy concentrating on breathing.

My neighbors were (surprise!) coke dealers. They were also (double surprise!) transvestites. But they were really poor, so they never quite got the transvestite fashion right. They would wear a muscle T-shirt, some weird jean mini-skirt, and workboots. They were like half-man, half-woman—transvestite centaurs. They also (triple surprise!) knew my ex-roommate Ernie.

We always had a steady supply of shady customers streaming in and out of the building. Once, I came out from my shower to find a guy trying to push a shopping cart through my front door.

He said, "Oh damn. My bad."

"Uh, that's okay," I said.

"Someone live here now?" he asked.

"Yeah," I said.

"Shit," he said. "This used to be our hangout." Then he wedged the shopping cart back out and wheeled it away.

———

My father called me and said, "Ah say, ah need to see a little California sunshine."

"Come on out," I said.

He came to visit for ten days. As soon as he arrived, he called my mother to tell her about my apartment. Just then, one of the sketchy coke buyers started pounding on my neighbors' door. "WILLY!" he screamed.

My father said into the phone, "Well, he kind of lives in a hut."

"WILLY!" the sketchy coke guy screamed.

"But it's got carpet."

"WILLY, YOU MOTHERFUCKER! I KNOW YOU'RE IN THERE!"

My dad said, "Goddammit! Will you tell him to keep it down?"

"What's going on?" my mom asked, over the phone.

"Nothing," he said. Then he went back to describing the property grounds.

I'd seen the sketchy coke guy before, hanging around the building. He looked super-insane. He reminded me of this Disney movie called *World's Greatest Dad* that I'd seen when I was six years old. He was a cross between the bad guy in the movie and Charles Manson. I know people always use Charles Manson as a description, but you know what? He really did look like him. His eyes were always open way too wide, like they were saying, "Heyyyyyyyyyyyyyyyyyyy." He looked like he'd just stuck his finger in an electric socket.

Because I wasn't in the coke dealers' union, I always kept my head down and never talked to my neighbors or any of their visitors. I didn't want to start now. But my dad kept insisting—and I didn't want to look like a chicken in front of him. I walked outside and said, meekly, "Excuse me, sir. Can you just keep it down? My dad's kinda on the phone. You know dads." Then I chuckled.

He looked at me incredulously. Then he walked into the coke den and got his drugs. A few minutes later, he walked out of the den and waved to me and my father. "Bye, fags!" he said, pleasantly. Now if it were up to me, that would have been the end of it. I was happy to have my manhood insulted and be put in the same category as Bruce Vilanch.

But my dad heard this and said, "What did that mother-fucker say? What did he say?"

"I think it was 'Bye fags'," I said. My dad decided that he was going to step up.

"Hold on Josie," he said to my mom. He put the phone down and went outside.

"Dad, I don't think you want to do this," I said. "This is Los Angeles!"

My father ignored me and instead went up to sketchy coke guy, who was getting in his car. "Ah say, mother-fucker. Ah say, what did you call me? What did you say?" he said.

The guy got out of his car, slammed the door shut and said, very slowly and deliberately, like my dad was deaf, "I. Said. BYYYYEEEE. FAAAAAGGGGS." His eyes were so wide.

He edged closer to my father. On his forearm he had this enormous, eight-inch-long, oozing wound filled with pus and scabs and matted hair. He was all wired from the drugs. And my dad said, "You want to say more shit?"

"Dad!" I screamed. "He's got gangrene, and he's from the fucking Manson family!"

The guy slammed his fist on the hood of the car and screamed, "I'll say any fucking thing I want, all right!!! YOU WANNA PIECE OF ME? C'MON, BOTH OF YOU!"

He got a foot away from me and my dad. Finally, my father said, "Jamie, this guy's crazy."

REALLY?

"C'mon you fucking Marys," Coke Guy said. "C'MON!" He was like a crazed animal. This guy would have eaten my father and me alive.

"Maybe we should go back inside," my dad said.

We went back inside. My mom was still on the phone, waiting.

"What's going on?" she said.

"Oh nothing," my dad said. "One of Jay's friends is out here, dancing."

"Oh, I love dancing! FUCKING QUEERS!" the guy screamed from outside.

"Sounds like a fight," my mother said.

"No, no fights," he said. "Just one of Jay's friends, tap dancing."

"FAGGOTS!" Coke Guy screamed. Then he got into a Volkswagen Jetta and drove off.

I thought, *We're faggots? Look at your car, bitch.*

Two hours later, we were eating at Burger King, and my father said, "I'll tell ya, that guy started to back off when I confronted him."

"Whaddya mean?" I said. "We wimped out."

"Hell no, we didn't wimp out!" my father said. "I told that honky straight up. He backed down. He left."

"Yeah, but we went back inside," I said.

"Yeah, but I didn't back down," he said. "Hell no. You backed down. You ran inside. I had the dukes up."

Out of nowhere, I heard someone scream, "This Whopper has no special sauce, you faggot!" I looked across the restaurant and saw Coke Guy yelling at a retarded cashier.

"Dad, there he is," I said.

"Oh shit," he said. "Be cool."

"Should we go beat him up, dad?"

"Shut up and keep your head down."

The guy threw his Whopper in the garbage can and swaggered out of the restaurant. Three minutes later, my dad said, "I'll tell ya, I could beat his ass." Clearly, a lot of Monday morning quarterbacking going on.

From Stoney to Scream

Because my hair was long, I was able to start filling the surfer guy/stoner/grunge rocker niche. Ron Leavitt, the co-creator of *Married With Children*, was casting a pilot called *Howe High*, which starred Denise Richards. The casting director saw me at a comedy club and called Peach, saying, "Ron was up late on Saturday night and came up with a character named Stoney." *Hmmmm* . . . She asked if I could come in and read for it. I did, and it was only the three of us. The casting director said, "Can you act stoned?"

"Yep," I said, and read the scene that way. They started to laugh.

"You really seemed stoned," the casting director said.

"Just acting," I said.

"Is it based on real life?" Ron asked.

I paused, then said, ". . . Yeah . . ."

They began to really crack up. Two hours later, they called and offered me the part. It was a valuable lesson—in giving people what they wanted. In reality, I had smoked pot maybe two times in my life.

After the pilot was shot, the studio decided not to pick it up. Soon after, Ron created another show called *Unhappily Ever After*. They brought over the character of Stoney, and had me back five times. This helped me out immensely. I was getting a regular paycheck and more recognition. The casting director of *Unhappily Ever After* also cast Ellen Degeneres's show. She had me meet the *Ellen* producers and I got cast in three episodes of *Ellen*. Suddenly, I was doing a guest spot a week.

———

It was time to try my hand at movies. I began reading the trades every day to find out what was being cast. Whenever I saw a part that might be right for me, I got the breakdowns from my friend Barry. Breakdowns are the lifeblood of agents. They are complete synopses of all the available roles in projects shooting around town. For example, Nicolas Cage might be making a movie about firemen, with a scene where he goes to the hospital for one minute. The breakdowns would specify the kinds of actors that were needed to play orderlies, nurses, people in the waiting room. Breakdowns are completely confidential and only agents and managers are supposed to see them. So if an actor doesn't have a representative, there's no way for him to get auditions. However, if an actor can steal the breakdowns or get them illegally, he can use them to crash auditions. Or an actor can read them after he already has representation, to see what his agent or manager isn't sending him out for. Barry used to buy these breakdowns illegally for fifty dollars a month and we had to go pick them up in a shady apartment in Hollywood. It was like doing a drug deal. This makes sense, since for actors, breakdowns are like heroin.

One day, I noticed that there was a remake of *Romeo and Juliet* in the works. I called Peach and asked, "Can you get me an audition?"

"Why do you want to do *that*?" she asked. "Shakespeare's so old."

After some persuasion, she got me in. They had me come in three times. After my last callback, the director, Baz Luhrman, asked me, "How did that feel?"

"I thought it felt pretty good," I said.

He said, "I thought it felt good too."

I didn't hear anything for the next three months.

Just after Thanksgiving, I got a call from Peach. "YOU GOT THE OFFER!" This was so much better than living in my car.

I had two and a half months to prepare. I locked myself in

my apartment and practiced my accent. The original plan was to have my character, Sampson, and another character, Gregory, talk like Beavis and Butthead. (Theme!) They nixed that idea pretty quickly.

Before I left LA, I auditioned for a Wes Craven project called *Scary Movie*, which was later retitled *Scream*. I saw the description in the trades and felt this weird kinship to the movie. I immediately went through the breakdowns and saw a character named Randy, a lanky fifth-wheel type. I circled it and said, "I'm going to get this part." Now I said that a lot, but this time I really felt it in my heart. There was something different.

I called Peach. She said, "Honey, you've been submitted already."

I didn't believe her. "Submitted?" I said. "Can you get me an audition?"

She did. The script was different: scary, funny, smart, and very self-aware. I'd never read anything like it. Randy was a standout role—he was like the voice of the audience.

My *Scream* audition went well. I played Randy like a really knowledgeable, aggressive, Quentin-Tarantino-esque movie buff. The casting director, Lisa Beach, said, "That's it! Hi Randy, you're the guy."

"*Really?*" I asked.

"Yeah," she said. "You're the first person to read for the role, but I really think you're it."

"I totally feel that way too," I said. "But are you just saying that?"

"No," Lisa said. "You're the guy. Can you come back and read for Wes Craven next week?"

"Yeah!" I said.

Peach got a call that afternoon. They wanted me to come in and read for Wes the next day. There was all this urgency

MIRAMAX/WOODS ENTERTAINMENT
"SCARY MOVIE"
FEATURE FILM
UNION   PAGE TWO.

STUART Billy's sycophantic best friend and Tatum's boyfriend, he is a Billy wannabe -- almost handsome, almost the jock, almost cool -- but he tries too hard to succeed. Socially awkward, completely tactless and slow on the uptake, Stu teases Sidney about the new murders and about her mother's murder, as the anniversary of the grisly deed approaches. Apparently harmless, unsuspected of involvement in the murders, Stu eventually reveals himself to be Billy's equally psychopathic second-in-command, showing that Billy was actually able to commit the murders, in spite of his alibi, because he had an assistant. Stu, believing that he and Billy are invincible, helps Billy to bait and tease Sidney once they have cornered her in their climactic, bloody murder spree at Stu's house. While exposing their plan to Sidney, Stu is surprised by her resistance when she knocks him unconscious, finally shooting him in the head with reserved aplomb...LEAD (26)

RANDY The fifth wheel in Sidney's gang of high school chums, tall and gangly, a witty jokester who elevates being a geek to coolness, Randy does not aspire to be like Billy the way Stu does. Randy, who hides a secret crush on Sidney from everyone but Stu, is a part-time employee at Blockbuster and a diehard movie buff. Displaying a youthful, lurid interest in the new string of murders, Randy appears at Stu's school-closing party with an armful of horror videos, unaware that a real horror story will soon be playing out in the house. Attacked by the murderers, Randy startlingly reappears in the end, while Sidney and reporter Gale Weathers bravely overcome the psychopaths. Retaining his presence of mind in the face of horror, Randy remembers to ask Sidney to go out with him after she shoots Billy and Stu..LEAD (26) **ALL ETHNICITIES WELCOME**

GALE WEATHERS In her 30s, stunningly attractive, with long legs and a smart face that is overshadowed by her flashy smile and massive mane of chemically enhanced hair, she is an ambitious, assertive reporter for a television tabloid news program In the process of writing a book about Sidney's mother's murder, dreaming always of putting her journalistic talents to better use, Gale hovers eagerly around Sidney after the new, high school student murders begin. Sensing a story, Gale persists in investigating, although she must endure the hostility of Sidney and her friends, stemming from Gale's firm belief that Sidney bore false witness in the trial of her mother's accused killer Finding herself attracted to the sweet and helpful, boyish Deputy "Dewey" Riley, with whom she flirts liberally, Gale is accidentally swept up in the murder spree at Stu's fateful party. Tough and resourceful, surviving a serious auto accident, Gale ultimately surprises the killers, shooting Billy and saving Sidney LEAD (23)

DEPUTY "DEWEY" RILEY About 25 years old, a big guy with a well-developed, muscular upper body, charming and handsome in a clean-scrubbed, boyish way, he is smart-mouthed Tatum's beleaguered brother and Sheriff Burke's trusted, loyal main deputy Friends with his sister's pal Sidney, he worries about her emotional state on the anniversary of her mother's murder, especially after the murders resume and the mysterious, masked killer begins to stalk Sidney Strongly attracted to beautiful television reporter Gale Weathers he invites her to accompany him on his apparently routine patrol on the night of Stu's party, not realizing that a bloodbath will soon ensue. Attempting to protect Sidney to the end, Dewey is stabbed to death in the back by Billy...LEAD (25) *[Copyright 1996, BREAKDOWN SERVICES, LTD.]*

about it. I went back in the next day and auditioned for Wes. "Good," he said, totally pokerfaced. Maryanne, the producer, was even more pokerfaced, saying "Mmm hmmm." I got absolutely nothing from them. I thought, "Shit! I didn't even come close to getting this." This is what actors go through. You go and audition and then wait and cringe and freak out. And you never know what to expect.

I called Peach for feedback. She said, "Honey, I don't know. You have to go down to Mexico and do *Romeo + Juliet* now and just wait."

Two weeks later, I still hadn't heard a thing. So off to Mexico I went. From the start, the shoot was intense. I landed on what seemed like another planet. The culture, the rituals, the architecture, the religious statues on every street corner— Mexico City was like nowhere I'd ever been. The set was isolated from everything else in town. The weather was always changing—from sunny and 90 degrees to crazy rainstorms. Our shoot kept getting extended. I was supposed to be on set for three weeks and ended up staying three months.

I spent half my time there stalking Claire Danes's mother. Miramax was pursuing Claire to be the lead in *Scream*, so I thought, "Hey, if the studio sees that I'm being helpful, maybe they'll give me Randy." I sat next to Mrs. Danes at lunch every day, and tried to convince her that the part was perfect for Claire.

"Well, it's a lot of blood," Mrs. Danes said. "I just don't know."

"Yeah, but it's *fake*. It's all *fake* blood." I argued.

"But it's all about mutilating women," she said. "Why don't any men get killed in this?"

"It's not the same. Men aren't that sexy when they're screaming for their lives," I said.

She got up from the table and went to sit with the Capulets.

————

A few weeks later, I flew back to LA to test for a movie called *The Pest*. I was allowed to leave the set for twenty-four hours. Peach picked me up at the airport, and took me straight to my audition. While we were driving, she said, "Oh, by the way, Wes Craven called. He wants to see you for that *Scream* thing."

"When?" I asked.

"This afternoon," she said.

"What?! Why didn't you tell me?"

"I forgot."

"Jesus," I griped.

"Calm down sweetie," she said. "Here, have some coffee. I put a little Kahlua in it."

My *Pest* audition was not good. The director said I was doing a Berlin accent when he wanted a Munich accent, and I didn't get the part. From there, I went right to meet with Wes Craven and the producers of *Scream*. My hair was dyed bright pink for *Romeo + Juliet*. When I walked into the room, Lisa said, "Your hair! It's pink!"

"Yeah, it's for my new movie. It's *Shakespeare*!" I said, hoping to impress them with my new credentials.

"With pink hair?" Wes asked.

"Yeah, Shakespeare," I said. "You know—William?"

I did the scene for Wes and company, and they were very receptive. I felt good about it, but I didn't know. As I was leaving, Lisa's assistant grabbed me and said, "I have a good feeling about this for you. I can't guarantee anything, but I think you have a chance." My nerves were fried.

That night, I flew back to the set of *Romeo + Juliet*. Peach called me on Monday to tell me that I was in the top ten for *Scream*. The next day, she called again to tell me I was in the top six. The next day, she called again. "You're in the top four," she said. "They still like you." The day after that, she called and said, "HONEY! You're in the top two. This is a big deal now!" Later that day, she called me back and said, "HONEY! I think they want to give you this movie!" All of a sudden, we were best friends.

The next day, Peach called again and said, "Miramax just made you an offer!"

"REALLY?" I said.

"YES!"

I started to panic. *Romeo + Juliet* was *Shakespeare*. I started thinking to myself, *Do I really want to be in a horror movie? I mean, I'm speaking in iambic pentameter here!* Of course, what I was really doing was running around like a pink-haired monkey, getting hit over the head with a purse, and saying lines like "Peddler's excrement are you!"

I was freaking out over what should have been the easiest decision of my life—being a complete moron. Then, fate started making my decisions for me.

Peach called back in the morning. "Honey," she said. "They've retracted the offer."

I felt like someone knocked the wind out of me. "Why?"

"Wes loves you, Lisa loves you, the producers love you, but the studio wants to find a name actor."

"NO! WHY?" I said.

"Well, everyone else has film credits except for you."

"But I'm doing a film right now! It's Shakespeare! William!"

"Yeah, with pink hair, I know, I know."

"But I'm—"

"Oops, there's Cost Plus Liquor on the other line. I'll talk to you later."

Click.

———

Wes, Lisa, and Maryann decided to fight for me. Wes called the studio and said, "Look, Jamie Kennedy's our guy. He's perfect for this part." Miramax looked at my screen test again. Then, they reinstated my offer, which I quickly accepted. I left the set of *Romeo + Juliet* and started rehearsals for *Scream* a week later.

After the first table reading, Wes said to me, "I'm so glad we could get you."

"Get *me*? I'm lucky. Thank you for sticking your head out for me."

Without Wes, I might have never gotten my career off the ground. I always have him to thank for that.

———

I'd been ready for something to happen for so long, and I wasn't going to mess up this opportunity. Whenever I wasn't shooting, I sat in my hotel room and just ran lines, over and over. I know it sounds a little compulsive and unhealthy, but I was scared of forgetting a line, or not being funny enough. I wanted to prove that I was deserving of the risk everyone was taking on me.

Cut the Fucking Check

I had been with Peach for a year and a half at this point, and things weren't working out. It was partially my fault. From the start, I gave all my power away. You need to be a team with your representative, not their subordinate. But I was scared of

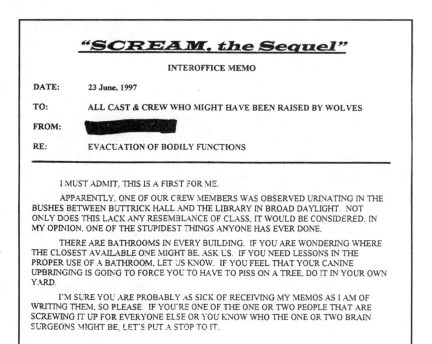

"SCREAM, the Sequel"

INTEROFFICE MEMO

DATE: 23 June, 1997

TO: ALL CAST & CREW WHO MIGHT HAVE BEEN RAISED BY WOLVES

FROM: ▬▬▬▬▬▬

RE: EVACUATION OF BODILY FUNCTIONS

I MUST ADMIT, THIS IS A FIRST FOR ME.

APPARENTLY, ONE OF OUR CREW MEMBERS WAS OBSERVED URINATING IN THE BUSHES BETWEEN BUTTRICK HALL AND THE LIBRARY IN BROAD DAYLIGHT. NOT ONLY DOES THIS LACK ANY RESEMBLANCE OF CLASS, IT WOULD BE CONSIDERED, IN MY OPINION, ONE OF THE STUPIDEST THINGS ANYONE HAS EVER DONE.

THERE ARE BATHROOMS IN EVERY BUILDING. IF YOU ARE WONDERING WHERE THE CLOSEST AVAILABLE ONE MIGHT BE, ASK US. IF YOU NEED LESSONS IN THE PROPER USE OF A BATHROOM, LET US KNOW. IF YOU FEEL THAT YOUR CANINE UPBRINGING IS GOING TO FORCE YOU TO HAVE TO PISS ON A TREE, DO IT IN YOUR OWN YARD.

I'M SURE YOU ARE PROBABLY AS SICK OF RECEIVING MY MEMOS AS I AM OF WRITING THEM, SO PLEASE, IF YOU'RE ONE OF THE ONE OR TWO PEOPLE THAT ARE SCREWING IT UP FOR EVERYONE ELSE OR YOU KNOW WHO THE ONE OR TWO BRAIN SURGEONS MIGHT BE, LET'S PUT A STOP TO IT.

Peach. I always thought she was going to drop me. Right after I signed with her, we got in an argument. It was the Friday of Fourth of July weekend. She said, "I don't know if I can work with you anymore."

"What do you mean?" I asked.

"You're too needy. I have my own life." she said. "Okay, gotta go."

"Wait! Are we still working together?" I asked.

"I'm . . . sssss. . . . going through . . . ssss. . . . a canyon . . ." she said and hung up the phone.

I couldn't get ahold of her all weekend. She had gone to Cabo, something about needing a vacation from Bel Air. I just sat in my garage, freaking out for four days. When I finally reached her, I was nearly hysterical. "Are we still working together or not?"

"Of course we are, honey," she said. "I was just PMS-ing. It doesn't mean anything."

I couldn't book anything for months. Peach said, "You need to focus more, work harder, be more professional." Then she took a week off in the middle of pilot season to get lipo-suction. She came back on a Monday. That Friday, I asked her if she had gotten me any auditions over the week. She said, "Oh honey, I made two calls, and no one called me back. But listen to this. I was at Morton's last night, and this agent asked me to jack him off under the table!" I thought, *An agent? At least jack off a producer.* Can you imagine a doctor doing that? "Hey, I'm ready to remove your spleen, but first let me tell you about this nurse I just went down on." I mean, yes, entertainment indus-try people are a little more casual than the rest of the country, but Peach was in a league of her own. Every single time she saw me, she gave me a kiss on the lips, even when it was totally unnecessary. "How was the dry cleaners?" SMOOCH! Her kisses were wet and always tasted like cabernet.

One time, I was out at her house late at night, preparing for an audition. "You're tired," she said. "You shouldn't drive."

"I'm fine," I said.

"Lupe's in Guatemala for Cinco de Mayo. You can sleep in her bed."

"That's okay."

"Well, if it's too cold in the servant's quarters, you can sleep on the couch in my room."

"No, I'm good."

She left, then peeked in again and said, "We could take a shower together." What?! It came out of nowhere.

After that, she invited me out for a New Years' Eve dinner.

It was me, Peach, and two agents from William Morris. They kept trying to grab her tits in between ticks of the clock. Ten . . . Grab! Nine . . . Grab! I thought, "I'm ringing in the New Year watching my manager get wasted off Stoli and preparing to get double-teamed." Three . . . Two . . . One . . . The ball was dropping on my career.

———

After I got *Scream*, I stopped being scared of Peach and started to resent her. Now that I was working, she had little incentive to be productive. She'd call me at four on a Friday and say, "You're doing great! Let's go split a pitcher of sangria." Peach meant well. She believed in me. She introduced me to a lot of people, and I got some good jobs with her. But I wasn't looking for a frat brother. I was looking for a business partner. It was time to move on.

I took her to lunch first at Kate Mantillini. "Do you want some pasta?" I asked, pointing to the menu.

She frowned at me. "What's going on? You've never offered me mostaccioli before."

I took a breath and launched into my little speech, "You don't want to be my manager anymore, right?"

"What? What?" she squawked.

"You don't want me calling you at all hours of the night. I'm annoying," I said.

"What?! What?!" she repeated. She was starting to sound like a cockatoo.

This wasn't going so well. I said, "Uh . . . It's not you. It's me?"

She shrieked, totally pissed, "Who told you to do this?"

"Nobody," I said, meekly.

She scanned the restaurant, looking like a frenzied madwoman. Then, by chance she spotted Sean Penn three booths over. "Did he tell you to do this?" she screeched. "Did that fucking prick tell you to do this? He did, didn't he?"

"What?! No!" I said. "I don't even know Sean Penn."

"You motherfucker!" She picked up a piece of focaccia bread and threw it in my face. "I should have gotten papers with you," she said. "Everybody told me to! I'm so STUPID! I thought you were a good person! You're nothing but another piece of Hollywood shit!" PHOOMPH! She hit me square in the chest with a breadstick.

"Peach, I want to explain."

She continued hurling starches at me. "I knew it, I knew it! I'm so fucking stupid!"

"I think you're smart," I said.

She got *pissed*. "JUST CUT ME THE CHECK! JUST CUT ME MY FUCKING CHECK, YOU FUCK!"

Everyone in the restaurant got really quiet and stared at Peach. Our waiter brought over the carafe of red wine she'd ordered. "I SHOULD THROW THIS IN YOUR FACE!!!" Peach screamed. She took a giant swig off of it instead. Then she stood up and stormed out of the restaurant, yelling at the valet to bring her car around. We hadn't even gotten our appetizers.

14.

The Experiment

> *There is no security on this earth,*
> *there is only opportunity.*
> —General Douglas MacArthur

Banana Boy

Over the next three years, I shot fifteen movies and three TV pilots. I was getting good parts in great films that were hits: *Scream 2*, *As Good as it Gets*, *Bowfinger*, *Three Kings*, *Enemy of the State*, *Boiler Room*. I even helped produce a little movie called *The Specials*. Then, I just plateaued. I wasn't big enough to get leads in studio films, but my agents told me that if I took too many more supporting roles, I'd end up being a permanent second banana. So I couldn't be a lead banana, and I couldn't be a second banana. I couldn't even be a plantain.

———

I was very frustrated. I'd been there at the outset of the teen movie craze and suddenly, I felt like I was being left in the dust. Everyone kept telling me, "It's just not your time."

I needed to reinvent myself. The thing is, I really didn't have anything making me stand out from my peers. I wasn't extremely handsome, I didn't have an amazing build, and I wasn't so intensely brooding that my eyes would burn right through you. I was funny, but so were a lot of other guys in Hollywood. When I thought about it, I realized that there were two things that made me distinct: I had absolutely no boundaries and and I could do accents. It was a start. But I didn't know how to translate that into a niche.

Then, my friend Josh introduced me to a producer named Mike. Mike asked if I had any ideas for television. I said, "I want to do something where I can do accents and have no boundaries."

"Anything more specific?" he asked.

"That's all I got, dude."

A week later, I called him up and said, "I think I have an idea. I want to do a hidden camera show."

He said, "I've always wanted to do that too."

BINGO.

I'd first thought of the idea for a hidden camera TV show in 1994. I was standing in line at a Kinko's on Sunset, watching this lady hollering at an employee, saying "You ruined my copies! Get your boss! Get your boss now, dammit!" The employee got the manager, who came out and said, "I'm sorry, ma'am. We are trying to help you here." She kept snapping at the manager, saying, "I want this man fired. I want him gone!" The manager was just blowing it off, giving her the standard response, "Well, we'll certainly look into it ma'am."

I was so intrigued. I thought, *How could this woman possibly get so upset over photocopies?*

After the manager went back to his station, the woman started gathering up all her copies, preparing to leave. She was all angry, mumbling to herself. I loved the drama so much that I couldn't let it end. As the woman walked past me, heading toward the door, I said, ". . . Oooh."

She stopped in her tracks and turned around. I just looked at the innocent employee with a stunned expression on my face. The woman ran up to me and said, "What? What? Did that asshole say something about me?"

I had her hooked. It was amazing—I felt such a sense of power. I said, "I'm sorry. I can't tell you."

"What?" she screeched.

"I can't get involved in your affairs," I said.

She got so angry—it was great. I was loving every second of it.

"What did he say? You have to tell me! What?"

I started speaking slowly, with major dramatic pauses. "Well . . . he called you . . . a bitch."

Silence. And then, pandemonium.

"GET THE MANAGER," she screamed at the employee. "GET HIM RIGHT NOW!"

"What's the problem?" the employee said.

"You called me a bitch!" she shouted. "How dare you?"

"No I didn't," the employee said.

"Yes you did!" She pointed to me. "This guy said you did!"

The employee looked at me, totally confused. "Why would you lie?"

I just stood there, silent. Watching. The manager came out and the woman started screaming at him. "Your employee called me a bitch! This guy saw it!"

By now, the employee was screaming back at her, "No I didn't! No I didn't!"

Back and forth, back and forth. Finally, the manager asked me, "Who said what?" Everyone turned to me, waiting for my answer.

All of a sudden, I had a burst of inspiration. I started thinking how great it would be if this were a scene in a movie or something. But if I were directing this scene, I would do it differently. Like, what if I were playing the manager and this woman said, "I want you to fire him right now."

And I would say, "You know what ma'am? You're right."

Then, I'd turn to my employee and say, "Larry, you're fired, you ingrate."

Back to the woman, "Are you happy now, lady?"

And just when she was feeling all vindicated, I'd have the employee break down and cry. Then, his wife would come in with their three kids, all of them moaning, "Daddy, we're so hungry."

He'd be weeping, saying, "I got fired."

The wife would say, "I'M PREGNANT, YOU BASTARD! WHY DID YOU CALL HER A BITCH? WHY? WHY?"

He'd scream back, "BECAUSE I HAVE CANCER AND I'M MAD AT THE WORLD AND SHE FREAKED OUT BECAUSE WE WERE OUT OF STANDARD-CUT TAUPE DOUBLE-SIDED BOND PAPER AND I TOOK IT OUT ON HER!"

Then I would zoom in on the woman's face, to see how she felt. Because in my mind, she'd caused the whole scene by making such a big deal out of nothing. I mean, it was *copies*.

My reverie was broken by the manager's voice. "Hey, buddy. Did you hear me? Who said what?"

Back to reality. The manager, the employee, and the woman all stared at me, waiting. If I had it my way, I wouldn't have revealed anything. I would have left the store and let chaos reign. But it was just too uncomfortable. I had spun a web and everyone wanted to hear my answer. Finally, I said, "He didn't call you anything. He just went back to working the register."

The woman said, "Why would you lie?"

"Because it was exciting," I said.

They all looked at me like I was nuts.

I felt this rush of adrenaline flood through my brain. I thought to myself, *I'm complete, I'm whole, I'm one with the universe. My work here is done.*

I went home and started thinking about what had just transpired. And I realized that more than anything else, I'm an instigator. I'm the court jester. I mean, if I were living in medieval times, I'd be the guy sitting next to the king, saying "Sire, where's your wife? I thought I saw her diddling Friar Tuck in Town Square." I just love to get people to show their real feelings when they want nothing more than to hide them. If I think someone is hiding something, I want to expose it and point it out and talk about it. It's more exciting than ANYTHING. I thrive on it.

I thought it would be great to translate this impulse into a show, but I wasn't sure what the format would be. I loved *Candid Camera*, but I thought they ended their pranks too quickly. And I liked the skits on *Saturday Night Live*, but they were scripted. I thought, *What if I had a show where I played a different character in each hidden-camera segment, to help sell the prank?*

———

I told Mike my idea. Two weeks later, he called me up and said, "I was at a concert with Jordan Levin, and I brought your name up. He likes you." Jordan Levin was an executive at the WB network (he's now the president) who used to watch me do my bad standup at the Laugh Factory. Afterward, he would always come up to me and say, "You're funny when you bomb. It's like . . . you have no boundaries. And I like your accents."

Mike said, "We should pitch him." We met at Jerry's Deli for breakfast and began developing our idea, outlining it on napkins. Three breakfasts later, we were ready to meet with Jordan. I got so mad in the meeting because Mike kept interrupting the pitch to say, "Hey, this is the part where Jamie does something funny." Then he would make me stand up and perform like a baby seal.

Jordan liked the pitch and asked, "Have you taken this to anyone else?"

"You're the first," Mike said.

Jordan said, "We'll call you in an hour." He did, and they bought the idea.

Right away, Jordan hooked us up with a showrunner, a producer directly responsible for overseeing the show. The guy was great, but we had time conflicts, so he left us to create *Spy TV*. I was bummed, but I understood. Then Mike and I started developing the show with Michael Davies, the executive producer of *Who Wants To Be A Millionaire?* After a month, Michael's plate got extremely full, so he had to move on. We were zero for two.

The deal was about to end and I was losing hope. Then at the last second, a WB executive named Mike Clements called me in and said, "I want you to meet with these guys, Fax and Adam."

"What kind of a name is Fax?" I said.

"I don't know, I think he's Dutch. But they created *Mad TV*," he said.

I had a meeting with Fax and Adam. I thought they were nice. They thought I was a heroin addict.

I'll let Fax and Adam speak for themselves here:

Adam: When I first met Jamie, he was slumped over on the conference room table, and I thought he had smoked way too much marijuana that morning. His hair looked like he put his finger in a light socket. And he was very sleepy.

Fax: We were warned that Jamie was often thirty to forty-five minutes late for meetings, but we were pleasantly surprised to find him in the conference room already. Jamie had sixty or seventy one-line ideas. He was shuffling through them incoherently. Rambling, from one idea to the next. The amazing thing is that these continue to reappear two years later.

Adam: No matter how hard we try to destroy them.

Fax: We were very skeptical after the first meeting.

Adam: After we left, we said to each other, "Do we really want to create a show for a junkie?" But we thought we would look at his tape. For some reason, the network was really pushing this guy. The first thing the WB sent us were these interstitial spots. They were just Jamie introducing shows, saying, "Coming up next—Sabrina! What a witch!" in a forced, cheery voice. It seemed like someone had a gun to his head off-camera. How were we supposed to make a show about that? I called Jamie's agent for a tape and he said he couldn't send it, because he just had one copy. I said, "Are you telling me that the network wants us to build a show around your client, and you won't even give us a tape? How will Jamie feel when I tell him that?" Finally, the guy said, "All right, I'll send it. But don't let anyone know I let it out." After all that, the tape wasn't even edited. It was just three hours of badly dubbed-together standup pieces.

Fax: The great thing about the tape was how well Jamie bombed. He didn't care. We saw that he had versatility and that some of his characters could work well in a hybrid sketch show.

The tape Adam and Fax saw was some of the shittiest standup you've ever seen—me doing comedy in clubs and coffee houses over seven years. I didn't give them a reel with my movies and TV stuff, because I really wanted this show to come from a place that was really *me*. I felt that although my standup material was weak, it accurately captured my voice and my outlook.

On Monday, I met with Fax and Adam again. They came in and started quoting stuff from the tape, specific lines. I was immediately impressed. These guys had actually gone home and watched the whole grueling tape? Nobody in Hollywood does that. People try to scrape by on half-assed efforts. Then they pitched their idea.

Adam said, "We want to call it *The Jamie Kennedy Experiment*."

Right away, I was taken by the title. It sounded like something I'd watch. Even if my name weren't Jamie Kennedy. Adam later said that when I heard it, I came alive for the first time. It was like someone plugged me in.

Fax said, "It's not like you'll just be playing jokes on people. You'll be creating believable scenes that raise a moral or ethical question, and putting real people in the middle. Letting their conscience decide what to do."

"You'll be like the morality police," Adam said.

I was immediately sold. Adam and Fax understood everything I was going for. They really got inside my head and saw what made me tick. They were the first people in Hollywood who I didn't have to spell shit out for. I could just give them the germ of an idea, and they would take the ball and run with it.

After a series of development meetings, we pitched the pilot to the network. We had a scenario where I would play an infomercial host who was hawking a product called the Instacooker, which could make a hamburger in twenty seconds. I'd have a cook-off, pitting the Instacooker against a regular barbecue grill, using two volunteers from the audience—one a real person and the other an actor we'd plant in the audience. As soon as the actor turned on the Instacooker, it would blow up. After he was whisked off to the hospital, I would claim that the product was still in the testing phase. Then, I'd ask for volunteers to do testimonials. After everyone refused, we'd offer them a hundred bucks—to see if they would do it. (When we did this actual bit in the pilot, we only had to offer people twenty dollars to get their testimonials).

We proposed a budget for the pilot. The network liked it so much that they came back and gave us enough money to do thirteen episodes. I had never been so excited in my life.

Two months later, we started shooting. For the first bit we shot, I had to hide in a closet. It was the only way I could stay in the room without the mark seeing me. After half an hour alone in the dark, I started to stress out. It was our first day on the set, and we didn't have a trailer, because our budget was so small. We didn't have a dressing room, because we had to be stealthy. Our network was the WB, which didn't do any reality TV at the time. And people loved to shit on reality TV, especially hidden camera shows, saying, "They're just a fad. They're already played out." I worked myself up into near hysteria, thinking "What have I done with my career? Have I just made a huge mistake? If this isn't funny, I'm fucked. What kind of a name is Fax?!"

The bit revolved around a guy who our fake company hired as an employee. I played his boss. I went into his office and said, "Okay, your first job today is to fire some people." Then I left and sent in five actors posing as employees. After the mark fired them, these people went crazy, cursing and sobbing. The guy was miserable. I came back in the room twenty minutes later and asked him, "Hey, how's it going so far?"

He said, "Well, it's weird, because everybody hates me."

I said, "I know, but you're doing a great job. The thing is, we're cutting back right now, so I have to fire you."

He looked at me with murder in his eyes and said, "You're firing *me*?!"

"Yeah," I said. He was so pissed off. I could barely move. I thought, *Any second now, this guy is gonna lunge at my throat and throttle me.*

After about fifteen seconds of intense staring, I said,

"You've been X-ed. You're on a hidden camera television show, called *The Jamie Kennedy Experiment*," and he started to laugh. Thank God. After that, I wasn't nervous anymore. I had to get the first one under my belt to see what it would feel like.

Our show works like this. We start out in the writer's room. Someone pitches an idea. If we all laugh, we write the bit. Then, the producers set up all the behind the scenes stuff, from finding the marks to scouting locations. This is the hardest part, because it takes an unbelievable amount of work to put on a show like this, and we've got to sneak around and be stealthy.

It takes an entire day to load in the cameras and hide all the mics and the lights, to make everything look natural. We shoot each bit three times, so we have a choice of marks. Doing this is *so* different from film and television acting, because the other actors and I are performing opposite a stranger who has no idea that he or she is performing opposite us. Let alone starring in their own television show. We have to mirror their energy exactly, because they will totally bust us if we don't.

Revealing the joke always makes for a weird dynamic. Because five seconds ago, we were in the middle of the bit and I'm screaming at a mark for spraying poison in Jeff Goldblum's eyes. "Why do you hate Goldblum?"

He screams back, "I love Goldblum," and suddenly I go, "Hey, guess what, you've been X-ed! It's all a joke!" and hug him and try to make it all better. I always feel like such a creep. Even though the marks are usually very good sports about the whole thing, I always feel like they hate me.

Every once in a while, the marks freak out. One time I had a guy call me a Hollywood douchebag and storm off the set. Another time we did a joke where we set up a woman who performed as a clown. She wouldn't sign the release. She said, "I don't want to be portrayed as an idiot. It would hurt my

BROADCAST STANDARDS ACCEPTABILITY REPORT

To: ▓▓▓▓▓▓▓▓▓▓▓▓▓▓▓▓▓▓▓▓▓   Date: 1/23/02

From: ▓▓▓▓▓▓▓▓▓▓▓▓▓▓▓

Subject: **JKX**

ROUGHCUT NOTES: **Episode #3**   **E03.LOCKED0**   **1/22/02**

"Sopranos Pizza"
A reminder that it is necessary to completely wipe the audio on the underlined in "My balls are not gonna get cut off for nobody" (approx. 5:14). Also, the mark's dialogue at the end of the bit ("What the fuck/I'm gonna beat my brother's ass. I'm gonna beat his ass", etc.) needs to be completely covered by theme music as in the rough-cut. Please confirm that there will be no audio from the mark under the reveal.

"Birthday Party"
Approved.

"Brad Gluckman Golf"
A reminder that all material needs to be reviewed prior to locking picture. This bit was not originally submitted as part of this roughcut. We need to lose Brad's "wash my balls/keep my balls tight" in the tease before the commercial break. We also need to audio wipe Brad's "keep my balls tight" in the body of the sketch.

career." Once, we were doing a scene in an Italian flower shop and the actor playing my boss screamed at me, "ARE YOU FUCKING MY WIFE????" at the top of his lungs. The mark just turned around, ran out, and hopped on a bus.

The worst is when a mark cries. That's when I feel like a true jerk. It's usually not because they're upset. It's because they're so relieved that the whole setup was fake, because they didn't want to believe human nature could really be so awful.

It's amazing what people will believe. Sometimes I'll be in a bit with my nose falling off. People will stare at it and I'll say, "Oh, I have a skin condition," and nobody will question me.

The show is really my dream job. There's nothing better than going to work and laughing all day. It's like the perfect combination of everything I always wanted to do with my life. There's something so cleansing about the whole process. Every time I get an idea done and shot, it feels like I've exorcised some kind of comedy demon from my brain. I always wonder what I'll do if I run out of ideas. I guess just sit around not saying much. I'll probably watch more TV.

Malibootay

My love affair with rap music, hip hop culture, and black people in general began when I was thirteen years old. I used to play basketball at a playground called Keystone with my best friend David Haggerty, who we called Eggs, on account of his egghead. Keystone was your basic playground. There was a gang who used to hang there called The Sunshine Gang. I know their name sounds gay, but they were badass—Eggs and I were always scared of them.

Eggs was the only white kid on the playground who could dunk a basketball, so we both got in with the black kids.

From: Valerie Mullen< nival@aol.com>
Subject : Jamie "Lying Motherfucker Kennedy"
To: Jamie Kennedy jamiek@aol.com

Asshole,

May I please have the number to your representation?

We have worked on a site for in your name, for three years now, for no pay and have had to spend a lot of money on webspaces, domain names, etc. We are struggling actors and filmmakers (remember those days, huh?) who have a lot more to do with our lives and money than to be stepped on in the cyber world.

To be thrown away like this –without any notice, mind you—is a total slap in the face. We found out about the Star Street deal from some fan who had the decency to let us know what was going on. WE were supposed to be the "Official Unofficial" Jamie Kennedy homepage, not Star Street. Believe it or not we're not 13 yr old drooling fans. We run a business and take it as seriously as any corporate CEO.

We feel foolish that we did not put the Official, Unofficial homepage deal in writing. Because if we had, this CLEARLY would have been a breach of contract.

I know that you were behind this. And I hate you for taking our livelyhood. Keep steeping on the backs of your internet fans.

FUCK OFF!!!

Sincerely

-Valerie

P.S.

...AND IF YOU THINK WE'RE FANS "J". WE'RE NOT. JESSICA LEFT A LONG TIME AGO, BECAUSE SHE COULD NO LONGER STAND WORKING THANKLESSLY ON A SITE FOR AN ABSENTEE CLIENT. COULDN'T YOU WRITE BACK ONCE AND SAY " HEY VALERIE, NICE JOB." WE MADE THE SITE FOR YOU!!! JUST A LITTLE ACKNOWLEDGEMENT WOULD HAVE BEEN NICE. I MEAN IT WAS A SHRINE!!! ANY OUNCE OF BEING A FAN THAT WAS ONCE THERE, IS NOW COMPLETELY DRAINED OUT OF US.

WE WILL NO LONGER BE BOTHERING YOU. HAVE A GOOD LIFE!!!

Dear Jamie, I love you.
I watched scream 1 and
scream 2 and I was so
happy when you did
not die. I had a
hamster named Bubbles
and he died because
I hugged him too hard.

Do you have any pets?
I made a picture for you.

Do you have a
girlfreind?
ok I can't think of
what else to say
so bye.

Megan, Age 6 years
old

We became tight with a kid named Sean, who went by the name of Lump because he had a permanent lump on his forehead. One day, when we were all sitting around, Lump gave me a tape and said, "Yo son, hear this. This is the new shit." It was 1983. The tape was Run-DMC. I'd never heard of them and I thought this was the oddest name for a group. I was like, "Are they from the future? What is it?" When I put it on the radio and played it, I was instantly blown away. I had never heard anything like its infectious beats and pumping rhythms. The anger in its rhymes made me feel cool.

Before rap all I'd listened to was AC/DC's *Back in Black* and some Ozzy Osborne. I still loved them, but once I heard Run-DMC, it was on. I bought all the tapes I could find—the Disco Three, who were later renamed the Fat Boys, KRS One, Boogie Down Productions. Then came Bigg Dady Kane, Eric B & Rakim, and of course the Master, LL Cool J. I also started getting into Will Smith, who was only played locally. "Parents Don't Understand" was a big hit in Philly for two years before it went national.

I started to get deeper into black culture. I went to movies at the 69th Street Terminal, which was a real ghetto movie theater. There, I saw *Beat Street*, *Breakin'*, and *Krush Groove*. The movie theater was great because people would scream at the screen. I remember seeing *Day of the Dead* there and being more entertained by the audience than the movie. Whenever someone was about to get killed, women would jump up and yell, "YOU DEAD, BITCH! GODDAMN, HE GONNA CUT YOU OPEN!" They were really quite invested.

My friends and I also got into breakdancing. We would sneak into my garage and practice our popping and locking for hours. I did the worm. I wore parachute pants and was persecuted for it. My love of hip hop culture grew and grew. I became that kid from the suburbs who wanted to be down. But it wasn't until I moved to LA that things just got ridiculous.

When I was just starting out, I always saw this white kid hanging out at the Grind Coffeeshop right next to the Improv in Hollywood. He'd walk around saying, "Hey dog, you don't know me. I'm from the streets." When he'd order a coffee, he'd be like, "I need a venti decaf vanilla lizzate and make it with soy. I'm lactose intolerant, biatch."

One day, someone finally asked him where he was from.

"Manhattan," he said. "Upper East Side. 72nd and Park, fool!"

I said, "Are you serious?"

"Serious as cancer. Y'all don't know me," he said. "You don't know my struggle."

This guy made for an amazing character study, because he had no third eye watching him, telling how retarded he was acting. Right there, I grabbed my pen and wrote the phrase down. "I'm from the streets." It just grabbed me.

I thought the white rapper kid would be an interesting standup bit, but he'd have to be from somewhere else, somewhere even more ridiculous. I sat around with my friend Al, spitballing ideas. I asked, "Where would this guy be from? Beverly Hills?"

"Too obvious," he said.

"Brentwood?"

"Dude, no one's even heard of Brentwood." This was pre-OJ.

Then it came to me. "Malibu."

Al laughed out loud and I knew I had something. I went home and started writing out ideas. Malibu was a great place, but what would be his turf? Well, all the different beach communities. You could have the Palisade Pimps and the Calabasas Crips. Representing in the 310. This could be a kid who didn't have a ghetto, so he used the mall as his hood. He could say, "Yeah fool, I don't wanna see yo' ass in front of Baby Gap no more. Take yo' shit down to Wicks and Sticks."

I named the character Brad Gluckman and started doing him onstage—and he killed. This was back in 1991, and the only white rappers the world had ever seen were the Beastie Boys, Vanilla Ice, Third Base, and Everlast, so the character was still kind of new. I kept him around for a long time, but when I started getting movie and TV jobs regularly, I quit doing standup. So I had this character I'd developed and nothing to do with him. Then, I realized that it might be possible to build a movie around Brad. I'd never written a screenplay before, but I decided to give it a shot.

I took Robert McKee's writing seminar and learned a little bit about screenplay structure. Then, I sat in my apartment for weeks, trying to write an outline, but I couldn't get past the first two pages—I just didn't know what the story was. I started getting more acting jobs, so I put Brad Gluckman on the back burner.

In the summer of 1998, I got a great job on the movie *Bowfinger*. It was shot in LA, so I got to stay in town. Plus, it wasn't a very demanding shoot—I was getting paid to be available for the whole summer. So, I bought a computer and went back to work. This time, a friend of mine who had already written a few movies helped me work up a basic outline of the story. I started writing out a very detailed treatment and got up to fifty pages. But before I finished, I picked up *Variety* to see a story about an actor named Danny Hoch, who was going off to shoot a movie called *Whiteboys*, which was about a bunch of kids from the suburbs who wanted to be black. I was like, "Crap! Someone beat me to the punch." I abandoned the project and let my computer gather dust.

A year later, *Whiteboys* came out, but under the radar. For whatever reason, the studio decided to make it a limited release. I thought maybe Brad Gluckman still had a chance, so I started working on the idea again. At the same time, I got an audition for the movie *Go*, for the role of a white, wannabe gangster. I ended up losing the part to Breckin Meyer. I thought, *Well, now it's really blown. I'm definitely not gonna have my shot. This character's dead.* Then, that movie came out, but the character didn't end up being that similar to Brad. I resurrected the treatment, but I just couldn't get it right.

In 1999, eight years after I thought of Brad Gluckman, I met a guy named Nick Swardson, who was a stand up comic and screenwriter. I told him a little about the character and he said, "You should do it like this," and shot out a bunch of thoughts—a scene of Brad Gluckman in therapy, a sequence when Brad goes to Spago and then to Compton, a supporting character named "Ohshit." I thought he had a lot of funny ideas, so we started working together. We started writing an outline. Nick would always tire out, so I said, "I'll pay you ten bucks a page to write it." After that, the script just flowed out of him.

We went through three drafts before we started taking the script around town, trying to get someone to finance the movie. People really liked it, but no one wanted to make it. They said it wasn't commercial and I wasn't a big enough name. We almost got two million from a German company, but then the deal fell apart. Then we almost got it made with an American company, but that deal fell apart too. It just wasn't happening. After a year, we put the script back on the shelf.

Then, I started doing my television show. The first character I wanted to play was Brad Gluckman, because I thought people would really respond to it. I did and he quickly became a cornerstone of the show. Meanwhile, Eminem was becoming huge, so that opened up the doors for white rapper characters. So once *JKX* started doing well, my producers and I went to the head of Warner Bros. and pitched him the idea of a Brad Gluckman movie. They liked it, but thought the script needed a major overhaul and brought on Adam and Fax, the producers of my television show, to rewrite it. They ended up reconceiving the whole film, making it bigger, with a better story. They beefed up the supporting characters so everybody in the movie got laughs. A movie that's focused entirely on a character like Brad can get old in twenty minutes, but Adam and Fax took him out of the sketch world and made the movie stand on its own.

We got a strong director named John Whitesell, who was ready to run with this thing. Then we sent out the script. We didn't know what kind of response to expect from actors. We thought it was funny, but then again, it was a script set largely in the ghettos of Los Angeles, written by four white guys— would people be offended? The first person to read and sign on was Taye Diggs. I couldn't believe it. He was a legitimate dramatic actor and he wanted to do this comedy. I was jacked.

Taye's signing on helped us a lot, in terms of giving us legitimacy. Our next guy was Blair Underwood. Again, I was shocked. This was a little comedy and Blair was a renowned dramatic actor who had done some big time productions. Then, we had a reading and the casting director asked Ryan O'Neill to play the part of my father. He was so funny that immediately afterward, I told everybody, "We've got to beg him to do it." Fortunately, he liked the script and signed on too.

All of a sudden, everything started coming together. We got Bo Derek, Anthony Anderson, Jeffrey Tambor, and Regina Hall. One of the Wayans cousins signed up. Snoop Dogg agreed to do a little cameo. The cast and dates were set. Everything had happened within three months. It was crazy.

Shooting the movie was the most exciting and gratifying

thing I've ever done. For ten years, I had this guy in my head, so to finally get him on film was exciting as all hell. It was a crazy shoot, though—very physical. I know acting's not like a real job so I can't exactly complain, but it was hard, because half the movie is about black guys beating the shit out of me. I was constantly being pushed, poked, prodded, and tugged at. Plus, I was called Cracker—a lot.

I was always stressed and tired. The studio had taken a big chance on me as an unknown quantity at the box office— and a lot of people's necks were on the line. Plus, I was a writer on the movie, so I was constantly trying to come up with new lines and takes and different shots, which caused its own problems, since we didn't have much money to work with. Our director had the daunting task of bringing in the movie within twenty eight days, so every minute counted. We couldn't afford to go into overtime.

I've never been so involved with a movie before. I was there from conception to shooting to editing and now to the marketing and the music. The experience has been a serious learning tool—I feel very fortunate to have had the opportunity to learn from all the different masters of their trade.

As I write, we're a month away from releasing *Malibu's Most Wanted*, so almost everything is out of my hands. I think we made the movie as good as it could be, and I really hope you like the film. Because if you don't, then I better not see yo ass at Gymboree, bee-yatch!

Epilogue

I have always observed that to succeed in the world one should seem a fool, but be wise.
—Baron de Montesquieu

I never knew what I wanted to do with my life before acting. I had no direction. I had no idea that this was an option. When I was growing up, I just thought Hollywood was something you were born into. Or you had to be discovered. I didn't know that acting was something you could pursue or work towards, like any other job. I feel very lucky to have found it. I think that's all we can really ask out of life. The rest is up to us.

When I was trying to make it in Hollywood, the only guides I had were actors' autobiographies. I read stories about other people's struggles, and they helped me get through mine. Without them, I would have been lost. That's why I wanted to do this book. To let people know that success isn't magic. It's persistence.

I believe that anyone reading this book can make it. And it doesn't have to be in show business. I believe that if you really want to do something, you shouldn't give up. And if you ever feel like you want to quit, sit back and ask yourself, what else do I have to do with my life? Do you have time to follow your dream? You have all the time in the world. You have your whole life ahead of you.

Jamie Kennedy
Los Angeles

Acknowledgments

I've had a lot of help from many people, so this is going to be a long list. If I forget anyone, please forgive me.

First, I want to thank my collaborator, Ellen Rapoport. Six months ago, you picked up a pile of paper in my office and sat there for the next hour, reading rough stories and semi-coherent thoughts scratched out on tiny scraps of paper, laughing out loud. From that first night, I felt validated. Thank you for working so hard throughout this process; for writing thirteen hours at a time, and then taking my three A.M. phone calls; for pushing me to be as honest and forthright as possible; for helping me shape my voice, and weaving these ramblings into a cohesive narrative. You are a great sounding board, you have an original sense of humor, and you get me. I'm lucky to have you.

I must also thank all the people at Kensington Publishing for taking a chance on this book after it was turned down by twelve houses. I am especially indebted to my editor, Jeremie Ruby-Strauss, for giving me the freedom to say anything while mercilessly hacking away the fat until an actual book emerged. With comments ranging from, "**WEAK**!! Not a story!!!" to "Give me more honesty!", you always said what was on your mind and encouraged me to dig deeper.

To the amazingly hardworking team of people who represent me—you're not only my business partners, but also my family. Thank you to: Alan Nevins, for never giving up on the book when everyone told you I was too young to write a memoir. Joel Gotler, for taking the time to help with my deal, even when your clients included guys like Tom Clancy (also for introducing me to Kelly Lange and costing me three thousand bucks). My agents, Marty Lesack and Jason Heyman, without whom *JKX* never would have gotten set up, for their non-stop dedication to getting me TV parts and movie roles. My lawyer, Mitch Smelkinson, for always trying to squeeze an extra dollar out of anyone and everyone. My business managers, Michael Stern and Ed Gross—please don't run off to Ibiza with my measly earnings. Constance Schwartz, for getting me some Coors love. Jackie Miller and Nick Nuciforo for hooking me up with all the best comedy gigs around the country, even when I didn't have an act. *Wait, do I have an act now?* Deb Grimes, my road-weary traveling publicist, for putting up with me through everything, and still getting me green tea. Marcia Hurwitz, for getting me all the fun cartoons. Finally, Pam Kohl and Brad Slater, the original B-Rad and the Midge, my aces in the hole, for always taking any idea I have and running with it. For not laughing when I decided that I wanted to write a book, and instead simply saying, "Great, let's set it up." You always go above and beyond the call of duty. I feel so fortunate to have found you guys, and I don't know where I'd be without you. Whether you're setting up my movie, hooking me up with your dentist, or giving me a ride to Toshi's, you are truly my lifelines. Shut up, Doug!

I am very grateful to everyone involved with *JKX*; without it I would have nothing. To Fax Bahr and Adam Small for running the show with a strong and creative hand, for being open to any stupid idea I have, for letting me go as far as I want, for supporting my Nicholson impression, and for teaching me Producing 101. You feel my pain—then you laugh at it and then you turn it into a bit for the show. Hopefully, you'll get my suffering into syndication. To Mike Karz, who has the most even temperament of anyone in Hollywood, for being an honest, stand up guy, giving us the freedom to get as crazy as we can, and always being in our corner. To Brian Hart, who has one of the most unique senses of humor of anyone I know. To the writing staff: Gary, Matt, Keith, John, Josh, Rob, and Jason, for coming up with the most outrageously insane ideas week after week. To everyone behind the scenes, for making the show what it is—you're the engine that keeps us moving.

To all the people at the WB network, from programming to promotions to publicity, for giving me mad love. To Mike Clements, for bringing everything together and always being our biggest supporter. To Peter Roth, for always saying yes and sending me gift baskets. To Tal and Tracey, for being more like sisters than network execs. And of course, to Jordan Levin, for running the WB network with patience and a funnybone, and giving the show a chance to grow and find its audience.

And more thanks to:

Larry Little and everybody at Big Ticket. Dr. Fuchs for saving my life. Theresa Donohue, my first mentor, who encouraged me to pursue acting. Ginny Graham, for getting me my first job. Joann Baron, D.W. Brown, and Tom Patton, for teaching me the craft of acting. Kathy Messick, for shepherding me through some tough times.

Everybody who gave me those early jobs and took a shot on me when no else would: David O. Russell, Frank Oz, Baz Luhrman, Robin Lippin, Tammy Billicik, Ron Leavitt, Ellen

Degeneres, Pam Thomas, Danny Robinson, Andrea Pett, Maryanne Maddalena, Richard Potter, and especially Wes Craven, for jumping me into the game.

The cast and crew of *Malibu's Most Wanted*, especially John Whitesell, who put Brad on the big screen in only twenty-eight days, for being patient with me, even when he was running out of time and money. Nick Swardson who helped me develop the script. Craig Mazin, for saying, "Take him to the 'hood." Jeff Robinov and Greg Silverman, for letting us make the movie we wanted.

John Donohue, my soul brother on Planet Earth, who's been there for me since sixth grade. You see things as twisted as I do, and go further than I do to get a laugh. Thank you for being a real friend. "I got spurs that jingle jangle jingle." Chris and Bob for making me laugh—Capper! Matt Cullen. Chrissy Curtain. Nick "Gallon Of Cheetos." Barry Tracten, for being my partner in crime. Gimme! Al Berman, my first mentor in comedy, who thought Young Dumb was a Chinese comic. Brian Havens and Amina Runyan, for all your hard work.

All the peeps who encouraged me and looked out for me in the lean years: Gary Brussel, Eric Edwards, Mitch Parnes, Judith Shelton, Jeff Hawk, Bill Torres, and Jimmy Price.

Different people and places in my life who have shaped me into who I am. Jenica, St. Alice, Annunciation, and Marshall Road Field.

My cousin Pateen, for working hours on end, transcribing my journals and tapes and finding countless ways to cook turkey burgers.

Christa, for being the most generous person I've ever met, and for loving all of me—the good and the bad. You are a bottomless pit of affection. I don't know how I got so lucky. My brother, for looking out for me and hooking me up with dough when I needed it. My sisters, Rosie, Cynthia, and Mary, for instilling me with feminine traits, and making sure I understood and appreciated women. My sister Patti, for taking care of me since the day I was born, fighting my battles, making sure I didn't starve, and telling me never to quit. My father, the funniest man on Planet Earth, who always said my personality would take me farther than anything else and taught me that money is just paper. My mother, the hardest-working woman I've ever met, who told me life is all about actions, not words, and gave me my dedication, drive, and sense of morality.

I truly appreciate it.

Photo credits for color insert

Page 4, bottom: Photograph of *The Jamie Kennedy Experiment* courtesy of Big Ticket Television/Ed French Special Makeup F/X

Page 6, bottom: Courtesy of Kadu Lennex

Page 9: Courtesy of the National Lampoon

Page 13, left: Photograph of *The Jamie Kennedy Experiment* courtesy of Big Ticket Television/Ed French Special Makeup F/X
Page 13, right: Photograph of *The Jamie Kennedy Experiment* courtesy of Big Ticket Television/Ed French Special Makeup F/X

Page 14, top: Courtesy of Jim Frees Photography, Las Vegas
Page 14, bottom left: Courtesy of Big Ticket Television
Page 14, bottom right: Photograph of *The Jamie Kennedy Experiment* courtesy of Big Ticket Television/Ed French Special Makeup F/X

Page 15, top: Courtesy of P. R. Brown
Page 15, bottom: *Malibu's Most Wanted* copyright 2003 Lonely Film Productions GmbH & Co. KG, All Rights Reserved

Page 16: *Malibu's Most Wanted* copyright 2003 Lonely Film Productions GmbH & Co. KG, All Rights Reserved

All other photos courtesy the author's personal collection.

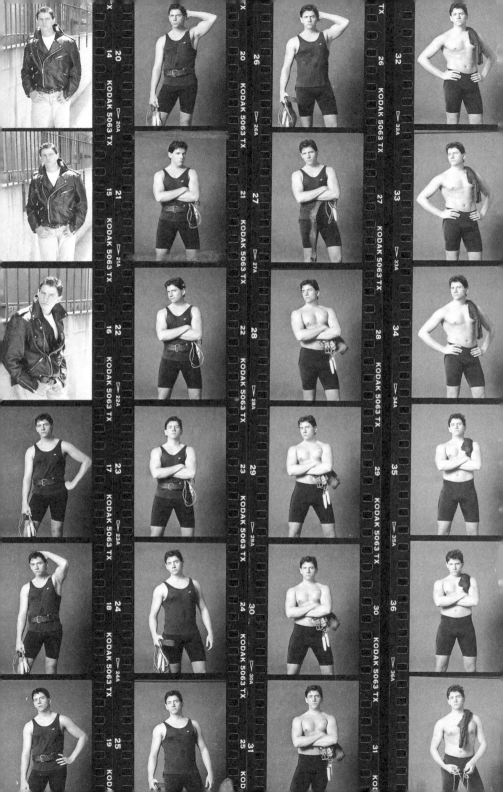